Harold M. Schulweis

Evil and the Morality of God

Hebrew Union College Press
Cincinnati 1984

Library of Congress Cataloging in Publication Data

Schulweis, Harold M.
Evil and the Morality of God

(Jewish perspectives, ISSN 0740-1582; 3)
Bibliography: p.
Includes index.
1. Theodicy. 2. Good and evil. I. Title. II. Series.
BL216.S38 1983 214 83-18659
ISBN 0-87820-502-0

Designed by Noel Martin
Manufactured in the United States of America
Distributed by KTAV Publishing House, Inc.
New York, New York 10013

Jewish Perspectives

1. Eugene Mihaly, *A Song to Creation: A Dialogue with a Text*
2. Sheldon H. Blank, *Prophetic Thought: Essays and Addresses*
3. Harold M. Schulweis, *Evil and the Morality of God*

To Malkah and Our Children,
Seth, Ethan and Alisa

Contents

Foreword

The Gothic word "evil" refers to the force in the universe that gives rise to wickedness, sin, misfortune, disaster. The presence of evil, its reality, makes a hole in the heart of the believer. We need God in order to "flatten out the abrasive edges of life," as Harold Schulweis puts it in this book -- in short, in order to live. But what are we to make of a God who too often seems helpless in the face of those edges -- indeed, seems Himself to founder upon them? To deny God is to open the doors of the mind and heart to the probability of cosmic indifference or chaos; to affirm God is to confront daily the need to understand the reason for suffering mankind. How do we respond to this dilemma?

Ancient man tended to regard misfortune as resulting from cultic neglect in his worship of the gods. A Hittite king once searched long and hard through his records in order to uncover the error that might have angered the gods and brought on the plague that was killing his people. For the early Israelites, suffering, individual and collective, was the result of violations of the covenantal stipulations; later, for the prophets, it was linked to moral blindness. The ancients gazed upon the world with open eyes and saw clearly the horrors that often shadow our lives. But theirs was a God-filled, God-dominated universe: the cosmos worked; when it didn't, the cause was clearly man's. "Shun evil and do good," urged the Psalmist, "and you shall abide forever. For the Lord loves what is right, He does not abandon His faithful ones.... But transgressors shall be utterly destroyed, the future of the wicked shall be cut off."

Between the covenant of Moses and the cry of Job lie a thousand years of biblical religion. For the author of the Book of Job the covenantal relationship of reward and punishment seemed no longer to be functioning. Perhaps that author was witness to the decades of slaughter visited by Syrian Hellenizers upon Jews faithful to the covenant. Or perhaps he looked at the world with suddenly keen new eyes and stated bravely what others had dimly sensed and had been fearful of saying: God is no longer holding to the terms of the covenant.

The breakdown of the covenantal relationship elicited three fundamental responses in the Second Temple period: (1) the Jobian answer asserted that suffering was not necessarily the result of covenantal violations by man, that the cosmos as a totality made sense, and that the reason for the seemingly indifferent manner in which the good and the wicked are punished is known to God but is bewildering to us because of our finite intelligence; (2) the messianic response deferred to a later time the reward for adherence to the covenant; (3) the apocalyptic response was an assurance that in a time soon to come all would be righted by a sudden cataclysmic intervention of divine power into human affairs. The second response became the heart of Pharisaic Judaism; the third response became the driving force of early Christianity. Both have endured until our time -- until Auschwitz, Dachau, Hiroshima, Nagasaki, and the general ambience of secularism which makes disbelief an easily acceptable contemporary position and a powerfully tempting alternative to strained dialogues with a blindly punishing deity.

It is at this point that Harold Schulweis begins his book. This is a highly sophisticated work of theodicy (a word coined by Leibniz, which means God's justice). Schulweis reminds us of Whitehead's wise warning: "Seek simplicity and distrust it." Much of the problem of evil comes from the very nature of monotheism and its postulates. Confronted with cool logic and remorseless evil, we must sacrifice one or another of these conflicting propositions: God is omnipotent; God is all good; God is wholly moral. "Therein lies the failure of the major traditional and modern theodicies," writes Schulweis. "It remains one of the chief sources of contemporary religious discontent."

In careful and sometimes technical language, which the educated layman who reads with seriousness ought to be able to follow, Schulweis examines the strengths and weaknesses in the theodicies of Maimonides, Aquinas, Whitehead, Tillich, Barth, Buber, and others. Always his tone is respectful, his arguments trenchant, his dissatisfaction made painstakingly clear. We are patiently led to a new possibility in the way we might relate to the nature of evil -- to a predicate theodicy.

"The aim," writes Schulweis, "is not to prove the existence of the Subject but to demonstrate the reality of the predicates.... The critical question for predicate theology is not 'Do you believe that God is merciful, caring, peace-making?' but 'Do you believe that doing mercy, caring, making peace are godly?'"

The implications of this position are carefully explored in terms of the nature of the predicates (are they real?); where the predicates reside (if not in a Subject); whether or not the predicates form a unity; how they answer the questions "Why did it happen?" and "Why me?"; and what the predicates mean with regard to the nature of ungodliness, the act of prayer, God and history, and other traditional religious concepts. Schulweis candidly admits that this theodicy is not for everyone. "It is for those who are embarrassed by the theological rationalizations which leave God morally defenseless and turn Him into less than a moral being."

One might agree or disagree with Schulweis's preferred resolution, but one will certainly be taken with his keenness of intellect, the closeness of his reasoning, the quiet passion in his search. This book is a mirror of modern religious man on a sacred quest for an answer to one of the oldest of questions: the haunting and bewildering problem of evil.

Chaim Potok

Preface and Glossary

In Nathaniel West's *Miss Lonelyhearts* a character who writes a column for the lovelorn receives the following letter.

> Dear Miss Lonelyhearts --
>
> I am sixteen years old now and I don't know what to do and would appreciate it if you could tell me what to do. When I was a little girl it was not so bad because I got used to the kids on the block makeing fun of me, but now I would like to have boyfriends like the other girls and go out on Saturday nites, but no boy will take me because I was born without a nose -- although I am a good dancer and have a nice shape and my father buys me pretty clothes.
>
> I sit and look at myself all day and cry. I have a big hole in the middle of my face that scares people even myself so I cant blame the boys for not wanting to take me out. My mother loves me, but she cries terrible when she looks at me.
>
> What did I do to deserve such a terrible bad fate? Even if I did do some bad things I didnt do any before I was a year old and I was born this way. I asked Papa and he says he doesnt know, but that maybe I was being punished for his sins. I dont believe that because he is a very nice man. Ought I commit suicide?
>
> Sincerely yours,
> "Desparate"

Social and individual holocausts leave in their wake the most painful and profound of human questions: "Why us?" "Why me?" Few people in our culture have not asked that very question. In academic circles the question is subsumed under the problem of evil, and in theology it has given rise to theodicy, that branch which seeks to justify God's providence by reconciling His goodness and power with the reality of evil. The problem of evil can be simply stated, and even the answers can be put forth simply, except that the answers seem always to raise still more complex questions. We grab hold of a weed only to discover after much pulling that we have the longest and thickest root in our hands, one that extends far beyond the area in which it first appeared. In dealing with theodicy we are well counseled by Whitehead: "Seek simplicity and distrust it."

In our essay we have sought to organize and analyze the major strategies of Western theodicies and the widely felt disappointment with their solutions. We have traced the roots to a common theological conceptualization of God and His relationship with the universe which sows the seeds of its own moral collapse. Our own proposal for theological reconstruction is offered in the belief that theological progress can be made only if we dare grapple with the so-called perennial problems of religious thought.

Dealing with this sort of problem necessitates the use of some philosophic and theologic vocabulary. For those who deal with this subject matter, such technical language is a shorthand facilitating communication. For the larger audience of intelligent laity, such jargon may present more of a hindrance than a help. The brief glossary of terms which follows will hopefully assist the reader in understanding the arguments of our presentation.

Glossary

Altruism - a term coined by August Compte which has come to mean the pursuit of the good of others as opposed to egoism.

Apodictic - expressing necessary or absolute certainty.

Axiological - pertaining to value and the theory of value.

Dialectic - for Hegel, the process of change in which an entity passes over into and is preserved and fulfilled by its opposite.

Dualism - the view which holds that two ultimate and irreducible principles are necessary to explain the world, e.g., the good and bad principles of Mithraism. Cf. *monism*: the view that everything is reducible to one kind of thing.

Empirical - Gr. *emperikos* -- "experienced." Having reference to actual facts; relating to experience.

Epistemology - Gr. *episteme* -- "knowledge" + *logos* -- "theory." The branch of philosophy which investigates the origin, methods, and validity of knowledge.

Eschatology - Gr. *ta eschata* -- "death." That part of theology dealing with the last things; e.g., death, heaven and hell, the end of the world, afterlife.

Evil - Some philosophers differentiate three types of evil:

(a) Natural evil -- evils which originate independent of human actions; e.g., hurricane, drought, earthquake.

(b) Moral evil -- evil that human beings originate; cruel and unjust thoughts and deeds.

(c) Metaphysical evil -- evils originating in consequence of the finitude and limitation within the created universe; e.g., it is in the nature of things that lions are carnivorous and lambs herbivorous.

Hypostatis - A Greek word signifying that which stands under and serves as a support.

Monism - (Greek, *mones* = single) - the view that everything can be reduced to one singular kind of thing or that one principle of explanation (e.g., materialism or spiritualism) is sufficient to explain everything.

Noetic - those concepts conceived by reason alone. Those aspects of reality knowable by reason.

Ontology - (Greek, *ontos* = being, and *logos* = theory) - when we ask, for example, what is the ontological status of the idea of God, we inquire whether God is real or illusory, whether it depends upon our mind or exists independent of our mind.

Reify - to regard something abstract as a concrete or material thing.

Teleology - Gr. *telos* -- "end, goal" + *logos* -- "theory." The view that holds the universe to be designed.

Theodicy - Gr. *theos* -- "God" + *dike* -- judgment, justice." Usually the defense of God's goodness and justice in the face of the fact of evil. Cf. *anthropodicy* -- the defense of man's capabilities to will, act, and know in the face of evil.

Introduction: The Problem of Evil as an Internal Religious Conflict

True depths of tragedy become apparent when two equally divine principles come into conflict.

--Nicholas Berdyaev

We have come to know things "so unheard of and so staggering that the question of whether such things are in any way reconcilable with the idea of a good God has become burningly topical. It is no longer a problem for experts in theological seminars, but a universal religious nightmare."[1] Jobian boils have reappeared in our times more massively spread than before. It is now the comforters, not Job, who feel constrained to place their hands upon their mouths in disbelief.

The loss of faith in a benevolent, providentially directed universe remains a major concern of contemporary theologians. No one can doubt the multidetermined causes of the collapse of faith in transcendence. But typically they are traced to factors emanating from sources outside the circle of faith. After-the-death-of-God (*post-mortem dei*) analyses point outwards to Copernican astronomy, Darwinian biology, Freudian metapsychology, Marxist ideology, higher biblical criticism, and technocratic cultural biases as the external forces leading to modern disbelief.[2] Far less attention is paid to the internal crises dwelling within the matrix of monotheistic faiths, specifically those that are engendered by the problem of evil. These are more devastating to traditional faith than the challenges from without.[3] The implosion sparked by the holocaustal events of our century has exposed serious cracks within the monotheistic faith system itself. Not that the outcry of innocence in the face of genuine evil is new. But the cultural environment in which it is heard is new. In a traditional society the murmurings of Job could be smothered by theodicies attributing hidden sins to man and inscrutable ways to God. In a society open to other alternatives besides acquiescence to the mystery of God's ways and promises of a happy epilogue, repressed resentments against traditional theodicies burst out afresh. There is nothing new under the sun except the changing ambience itself. The spirit of secularity provides a new atmosphere for old doubts. We understand secularity to be not the substantive reason for the breakdown in faith but the enabling condition of disbelief. "Modern unbelief," Martin Marty has written, "represents originality not in the sense of surprise but as the decisive culmination of a century's long process of secularization."[4] The presence of evil in a universe created by a benevolent God who is the single ground of all being is indeed an ancient problem. The familiar scaffolding of traditional presuppositions surrounding the old questions has fallen. Under such conditions, old questions appear new and old answers must be reexamined anew.

It is not alone to the collapse of the scaffolding that attention must be paid, but to the structure itself. Why do the answers which theodicies offer seem so beside the point, and why do they appear so strained? Is it simply the complexity of the problem of evil which seems to embarrass the conscience of modern sensibility? Brand Blanshard has written, "the treatment of evil by theology seems to me an intellectual disgrace." Moral sensibility, as much as logic, is against such rationalizations of the destruction of innocence. "How can anyone of clean conscience call good in the Deity what he would regard as intensely evil in man?"[5] Our reexamination of traditional and modern theodicies will focus upon moral failures in the defense of God.

The Internal Crisis: The Presence of Evil

For post-Holocaust man, theological reconciliations with the spirit of secularity have not touched the raw nerve of modern unbelief. The postwar program of demythologizing the prescientific cosmologies of the biblical testaments, the exorcism of supranatural, unworldly divine activity, the replacement of the static categories of Greek metaphysics with those of existentialism or process philosophy -- none of these has dispelled the Nietzschean mood which clings to modernity. Disenchantment and incredulity remain, well after the warfare between science and religion has been called off. Could it be, then, that the locus of unbelief lies elsewhere? Could it be that the major irritants of traditional faith lie within the corpus of monotheism itself?

Three authors, writing independently of each other, have touched upon evil as a major internal problematic. In reviewing the epochs of man's homelessness which mark the dissolution of the classic relationship between man and the universe, Martin Buber refers to the image of the universe which "breaks up from within." Buber draws attention to the internal collapse of cosmological security "through the soul's experience of the problem of evil in its depth and through its depth and through its feeling of being surrounded by a divided universe."[6] This internal form of crisis is contrasted with the breakup of the unified universe brought about through the external impact of the scientific cosmos.

Hans Jonas suggests an internal conflict both in gnosticism and Heidegger's form of existentialism. The kinship between contemporary nihilism and the "anthropological acosmism" of the gnostic temper leads him to conclude that "it is not necessarily modern physical science alone which can create such a condition."[7] It is too simplistic to lay the cause of cosmic impiety and alienation at the feet of depersonalizing science and secularity. Clearly, the first three centuries of the Christian era were devoid of anything resembling modern scientific thought and physical science. Yet, Jonas argues, "the same kind of catastrophic devaluation or spiritual denudation of the universe" that characterizes our contemporary nihilism was evident in gnosticism.[8]

Max Weber reported the results of a questionnaire submitted to thousands of German workers before the First World War. It disclosed the telling fact that "their rejection of the God-idea was motivated not by scientific arguments, but by their difficulty in reconciling the idea of providence with the injustice and imperfection of the social order."[9]

All three citations refer to crises of faith brought about by an internal problematic and specifically by the experience of evil. Yet, for a variety of reasons, contemporary theology cast its eyes elsewhere to search for the cause and remedy of the religious breakdown. In this it was misled. *For most people, the breaking point of traditional monotheistic belief lies not in Darwin or Einstein, but in Dachau and Hiroshima.*

If the earthquake at Lisbon in the eighteenth century could have shaken the optimism of man, what should be expected from the widespread holocaustal ruins of the twentieth in which the destiny of others threatens to become our own? No challenge to traditional faith attacks every aspect of religious belief and conduct as thoroughly as the one fell blow from the hammer of gratuitous evil. The foundation and superstructure of monotheistic faith are jolted: the reality of the attributes of divinity, the meaning of providence and history, the significance of miracle, and the relevance of prayer are all shaken by the attack. The jarring presence of evil threatens the unity of the monotheistic mold. Its theodicies expose brooding dualisms too contrary to be reconciled by the dialectic of paradox and polarity.

Appealing to God's mysterious ways will not assuage the disillusionment born of the shattered promise of the governing moral God of the Bible and liturgy. Tillich has admonished contemporary theologians that people in "boundary situations" will not accept the escape into the divine mystery in view of the daily experience of the negativity of existence. "If theology refuses to answer such existential questions, it has neglected its task."[10] That theology can no longer address its classical theodicies to the survivors of the Holocaust need by no means spell the death of God. It may suggest that tradition has upheld an inadequate image of divinity. Out of the inner contradictions tearing at the heart of traditional faith, as revealed by the experience of evil, a new incentive for theological reconstruction may be born. Two or more conflicting ideas rubbed together in opposition may kindle new energy for religious renewal. This new power is "nothing less than the force of extreme despair, a despair so elemental that it can have but one of two results: the sapping of the last will of life, or the renewal of the soul."[11]

The evil we have witnessed is radical. No patchwork will cover its agony. Theology will either endure the pain of God's death or discover within the catastrophe a truer image of His divinity -- one, at any rate, which is worthy of belief.

Evil within the Context of Monotheism

We propose to examine the failure of traditional theodicies to respond convincingly to the Jobian distress reborn in our times. To do so properly requires theological analysis of those critical presuppositions of monotheistic faith which provide the parameters of the problem of evil. Theologians and philosophers of religion have tended to isolate the problem of evil from its wider faith context. Logically, the problem of evil is reduced to an alleged contradiction within three propositions, a combination of any two of which renders the third false.

1. God is omnipotent.
2. God is all-good.
3. Evil exists.

Given such a *Fragestellung*, philosophical theodicy is led to propose semantic qualifications of key predicates. God's "omnipotence," "omniscience," and "freedom" turn out to be more restricted than initially understood. "Good" and "evil" are given meanings quite different from their normal moral connotations. Having extricated the problematic from the body of faith, many theologians undertake their defense oblivious to the consequences of their ad hoc solutions for the remaining corpus of monotheism. They cannot understand the dissatisfaction of the believer with their solutions. Their "logodicies" (Cassirer) ignore the holistic character of monotheistic faith. They have segregated the problem of evil from the deeply held ideals of divine perfection which make up the monotheistic belief. Like the caricatured medical specialist concerned solely with those maladies falling within his particular domain, without regard to the treatment's effect on the whole organism, many writers on theodicy treat the problem of evil as if it stood unrelated to the organismic complexity of monotheistic faith. Theological surgery is performed and parts removed from the corpus of an organic faith without informing the believing patient of the losses he has sustained by such correction. Stephen Toulmin has observed that over matters of faith, one does not believe or disbelieve individual presuppositions: one accepts or rejects complete notions.[12]

Intrapersonal Conflicts

Examination of the constituent elements of monotheistic faith is necessary if we are to grapple with the intrapersonal character of the problem of evil. Unlike many other problematic areas, the problem of evil cannot be understood as if it were an interpersonal conflict between two or more persons. C. L. Stevenson, for example, divides interpersonal ethical conflicts into disagreement of belief and disagreement of attitudes.[13] He traces the conflicts to the separate backgrounds, interests, temperaments, and intellectual capacities of contending parties. In contrast, the Jobian conflict emerges from within one and the same person. His beliefs and attitudes are of one piece. No alien beliefs or background explain the inner discord raised by his experience of evil. The tension rises from within, from an excess of preference, from an affirmation of ideals inherited from traditional belief which are upheld jointly and simultaneously. Before the assault of evil, the unity of faith falls apart. To attack the problem of evil without relating it to the internal matrix of holistic faith is to fall prey to the fallacy of misplaced concreteness. Theological analysis cannot ignore the major presuppositions of monotheism which have colored the problem of evil and shaped the theodicies of tradition.

Arthur Lovejoy, in his masterful *The Great Chain of Being*, cautioned that the doctrines or tendencies which are designated by *-ism* and *-ity* suffixes present only an appearance of singleness and identity.[14] Such admonition is particularly applicable in the case of monotheism, whose highly complex faith contains dispositions and claims derived from a variety of biblical and philosophic traditions. Philosophers and theologians have noted the diverse strands of theology which weave a network of commitment through the whole of monotheism. G. F. Moore, for one, is not alone in contending that ever since Philo of Alexandria and the church fathers of the second century, scriptural philosophy has translated the biblical notions of God's spirituality into metaphysical ideas of simplicity, unity, and incomprehensibility. Whether and to what extent this translation is successful, and whether alternate metaphysical correlations with biblical religion ought to be attempted, remains a central issue in theology (e.g., Bultmann, Tillich, Hartshorne).

The contemporary believer in monotheism, however, has inherited what appears to be a seamless conception of a single God to whom all sorts of attributes of perfection, metaphysical and moral, properly adhere. The ideal of radical monotheism, H. R. Niebuhr explains, affirms that "the principle of being is identified with the principle of value and the principle of value with the principle of being."[15]

Beneath the seeming harmony reigning between the metaphysical and biblical attributes ascribed to the single God lies a latent dissonance which the problematic of evil brings to the fore. For evil, in challenging the monotheistic claim to divine perfection, forces theology to produce an apologetic which exposes its bias toward either one or another pole of the idea of perfection: either the metaphysical or the moral idea. Invariably, the attempted exculpation of God defends a major aspect of perfection at the expense of another. Each type of theodicy is compelled to divest itself of some vital part of monotheistic belief in order to protect what it considers to be the more valued ideal. It is around that excluded aspect that the arguments and counterarguments of theodicy are centered. A study of theodicies reveals the tacit presuppositions of perfection which govern the conceptualization of the God-idea. Characteristically, it is to the unarticulated preconceptions of perfection that theodicies appeal. In comparing the major types of monotheistic theodicies, theological analysis may discover the strained nerve of monotheism which holds in uneasy harness metaphysical and biblical categories.

But the situation proves more complex. Even after the two merged traditions have been pulled apart, each forming individuated theodicies, the Jobian alarm is not silenced. For, as we argue throughout, a crucial moral ideal of perfection which adheres to both the metaphysical and personalistic theologies is forced to be sacrificed in the course of their justification. In biblically oriented personalistic theodicies, the moral meaning of God's goodness is catapulted to a point beyond human comprehension. In metaphysical theodicies, God's goodness is qualified out of its moral connotation. In effect, each theodicy requires a *sacrificium moralis*. Therein lies the moral failure of the major traditional and modern theodicies. It remains one of the chief sources of contemporary religious discontent.

Outline of the Argument to be Pursued

In the opening chapter we turn to some of the major motives and interests of *homo religiosus* which inform the affectively laden ideas of divine perfection. We identify and characterize two such basic religious needs as "the drive to know" and "the drive to be known." These motivating drives are the sources of two different implicit ideals of perfection. The latter find their respective fulfillment in the metaphysical and personalistic ideas of divine perfection. In Chapter 2 we examine some of the multiple functions of the perfection paradigms in selecting, organizing, and grading the attributes of divinity. We focus upon two major ideas of divine perfection which shape the character of metaphysical and personalistic theologies and theodicies.

In Chapter 3 we analyze some of the classic positions of metaphysical theodicy as represented by Maimonides, Aquinas, and Leibniz. This is followed in Chapter 4 by an examination of three contemporary metaphysically oriented theodicies represented by authors of process, naturalistic, and existentialist philosophies: Charles Hartshorne, Henry Nelson Wieman, and Paul Tillich. A common thread runs through their justifications of evil. Despite the differences between them, their tacit commitment to a metaphysical ideal of perfection subjects them to a fundamental criticism based upon their neglect of the moral connotation of divine goodness central to the liturgy and scripture of the monotheistic tradition.

With Chapter 5 we turn to the personalistic ideal and its role in the religious explanation of evil as presented in some of the relevant writings of Karl Barth and Martin Buber. Of particular interest is the use put to the term "personality" as applied to the divine subject by both thinkers. In their theodicy, "personality" allows them to assign a transmoral meaning to "goodness." Functionally this approach is similar to the metaphysical conversion of the moral connotation of goodness, and seriously alters the original God-idea to be defended. In our discussion of the strategies of personalistic theodicies we include John Hick's contribution. His is the most comprehensive contemporary response to the challenge of evil. Additionally, it is argued from the tradition of Irenaeus and the Eastern church, in contrast to the more usual approach of Augustine and the Western church.

We are led to conclude that theodicies typically dissolve the problem of evil by blurring the moral claims of monotheistic faith. The failure of traditional theodicies to adequately reflect the moral ideal in the God-idea which they defend suggests a major flaw in theological conceptualization. Theodicies are tied to theologies. All of the major theologies and theodicies of monotheism are subject-dominated. They refer to a separate being, process, or person concerning which speculations of intention and power are offered. Theodicies are thus assigned the task of defending the subject, whether characterized as "It" or "Thou."

To sustain the sovereignty of the theological subject challenged by the presence of evil, the moral predicates of divinity are, consciously or not, repressed. The need to defend God from moral criticism leads traditional theodicies to minimize the legitimacy of the complaint. The moral categories central to the protestations of the plaintiff are shown to be inapplicable to the subject. As a result of such strategies, the moral character of God is compromised in order to save the sovereign subject. The moral connotation of goodness is supplanted by amoral metaphysical or amoral personalistic meanings. What remains, after the theodicy, is a subject to which a set of metaphysical and personalistic predicates are attached but removed from their moral meaning and use in religious life.

In the concluding chapter, we propose an alternative to subject-oriented theology which would free theodicy from its role of exonerating the divine subject by denying the normal religious meaning of its moral predicates. Such a reconstruction would alter the traditional formulation of subject-predicate relationships by adapting an inversionary theological principle. The predicates of divinity are treated as the proper subject of theology, and God is understood essentially but not exclusively in terms of the moral quality of the attributes described. Godliness (*Elohuth*), conceptualized in neither substantival nor personalistic categories, characterizes the organization of qualities discovered in the transactions of man and societies with their environment. We discuss the consequences of such a predicate theology for the problem of evil, and particularly the character of prayer that such theological reconstruction entails. Predicate theology offers a radical alternative to the traditional subject conceptualizations of God, one hopefully more responsive to the spiritual sensibilities of post-Holocaust man.

Chapter 1

The Drive to Know and the Drive to Be Known

One can distinguish two ways of approaching God; the way of overcoming estrangement and the way of meeting a stranger.

--Paul Tillich

In one sense, evil need present no formidable problem. What others call evil may be observed and recorded non-judgmentally, with the objectivity of a seismograph. The occurrence of evil will create no hellish conflict for the adherents of Stoic cosmic pantheism, nor will it produce anguish for the followers of Brahmanic acosmic pantheism. Disciples of monistic philosophies may rid themselves of the problem of evil by seeing through its "illusory" distortions of reality. Naturalists may look at an unconscious universe with piety sufficient to laud its impartiality. "Shall we not cling to it [Nature] and praise it, seeing that it vegetates so grandly and so sadly, and that it is not for us to blame it for what doubtless it never knew that it did."[1]

The presence of evil is uniquely problematic for those found in the ethical situation of monotheistic belief. By "situation" we mean that state of involvement which Gabriel Marcel explains as "not something which presses on the self from the outside, but something which colors its interior states."[2] It is the inscape of the believer's faith which assigns meaning and passes judgment of good and evil upon events which others may regard with indifference. To deal situationally with the problem of evil calls for an investigation into the interior state of belief of the monotheist. What is the set of claims entailed by monotheism which sensitizes the believer to the problem of evil? What complex of faith-expectations colors the perception of the believer calling for theological justification of certain acts and events? Which ideals of divine perfection integral to monotheistic faith seem frustrated by events in nature or history? Analysis of some of the composite units of monotheistic belief is indispensable for an appreciation of the internality of the problem of evil and the required task of theodicy. It is the character of faith which determines what is evil, and within faith, it is the half-acknowledged ideas of divine perfection which determine the adequacy of any proposed justification of God's ways. We turn then to some of the characteristic human drives and passions which lie behind the implicit ideas of divine perfection and "secondary formulas" of monotheism, to those anticipations which William James claimed "fix our beliefs beforehand."[3]

The Twin Drives

Within the religious literature of monotheism two preconceptual drives inform the dominant ideals of divine perfection. For the purpose of analysis they may be separated into the drive to know and the drive to be known. Each develops its own ideal fulfillment expressed respectively in metaphysical and personalistic ideas of divinity. Both dwell side by side until challenged by evil.

In one of Pascal's *Pensees*, these polar drives of the religious man are obliquely referred to: "Engulfed in the infinite immensity of spaces of which I am ignorant, and which know me not, I am frightened, and am astonished at being here rather than there."[4] To be ignorant and to be ignored are two expressions of estrangement whose affirmative formulation is found in the religious aspiration for cognition of God and recognition by God. It is this double form of alienation which the *homo religiosus* of monotheism seeks to overcome.

The Cognitive Drive

Kafka, in one of his parables, wondered that Adam had chosen to eat of the Tree of Knowledge though he was free to choose the fruit of the Tree of Life.[5] It was this preference for knowledge over life, Kafka's exegesis continues, which marked the original blunder of man. An older Hebraic legend, however, explains that there was but one tree, known by two names, in the primordial garden. In choosing knowledge, Adam chose life.

Theological formulation of this mythic commentary is found in Maimonides' identification of two attributes of God. "Wisdom and life in reference to God," writes the author of the *Guide of the Perplexed*, "are not different from each other, for in every being conscious of itself, life and wisdom are the same thing."[6] Such an identification foreshadows the intellectualistic divine perfection, one to be emulated by man. The drive to know which motivates the ideal deserves greater attention as a major element in the religious quest.

A religious craving for knowledge is not limited to rational theology. Whether obtained through rational demonstration, divine grace, or natural light, whether the ascent be made by use of logic and speculative metaphysics or by mystic dialectic which ends in the higher knowing of not knowing (e.g., the *docta ignorantia* of Cusanus), the goal is a salvific knowledge which may achieve a noetic union with God. To know God is to find one's place in the *scala naturae*, in an intelligible universe not abandoned to caprice.

This metaphysical hunger Tillich describes as an "ontological passion" inherent in man, the being in search of Being. It is important to emphasize the passionate religious character of the drive to know so that we better appreciate its role in shaping the metaphysical idea of God and its defense in theodicy. Tillich identifies this grasping for ecstatic knowledge in the Platonic *eros* yearning for the Idea, the Stoic drive for wisdom, the Augustinian longing for truth itself, the *amor dei intellectualis* of Spinoza, the Hegelian passion for the absolute.[7]

Evidence of a growing appreciation for the religious significance of the cognitive drive within Protestant theology may be found in Tillich's own ontological theology, in the religious adaptations of Whitehead's process philosophy, and in theological interpretations of the later Heidegger.[8] But the *locus classicus* of the religious noetic drive which exalts knowledge as man's ultimate beatitude is in the writings of medieval theology. We cite Maimonides and Aquinas as two of its classic theological models. For Maimonides, the *imago dei* which establishes the bond between God and man is the overflowing intellect of God in man. This intellectual love is exemplified in a divine providence which is correlated with and proportionate to man's exercise of his intellect.

> For providence can only proceed from an intelligent being, from a being that is itself the most perfect intellect. Those creatures, therefore, which receive part of that intellectual influence, will become subject to the act of providence in the same proportion as they are acted upon by the intellect.[9]

In these few sentences we are offered clues to the salvational role of knowledge, and to the direction which its *imitatio dei* is likely to take. Understanding or wisdom, Maimonides' major attribute of God, foreshadows the type of theodicy likely to follow such an intellectualized version of providence. For this 12th-century theologian, the severity of the calamity befalling the righteous is proportionate to the length of time during which the afflicted righteous were intellectually indolent. Man neglects the exercise of his intellect and occupies himself with "the vileness of matter"; in so doing, the divine influence which guides men and unites them to God is broken.[10] Man's intellectual distraction causes God to hide His face. Consistent with this rationalistic conception of God's providential character and man's imitative goal, Maimonides will explain Job's anguish as an intellectual failing. While scripture ascribes virtue and uprightness to Job, Maimonides argues that nowhere does it say that he was intelligent, wise, or clever. "If he were wise, he would not have any doubt about the cause of his suffering."[11] Having exercised his intellect, Job would either have avoided some of the tragedy which came upon him or have found consolation in the knowledge that God's providence is not concentrated upon "an infinitesimal portion of the permanent universe."[12]

Metaphysical wisdom, moreover, would add the consoling perspective which comes from knowing that the purpose of creation is not for the sake of man but refers, rather, to the will of God. The lesson is clear. Men who would enter into the class of prophets and seek entry into the "innermost court" of the divine palace ought to turn to the study of logic, physics, and metaphysics to derive proof for the existence of God and His conduct of the universe.[13] Knowledge of the structure and order of the universe brings the believer-philosopher to God. Faith is the consummation of the intellectual process. "For belief is only possible after the apprehension of a thing; it consists in the conviction that the thing apprehended has its existence beyond the mind [in reality] exactly as it is conceived in the mind."[14]

Thomas Aquinas shares a similar religio-metaphysical disposition. From Aristotle's assumption that "man by nature desires to know," he derives a divine purpose for such a universal appetite. The natural desire to know leads man to probe into the cause of all things. In the process he discovers the ontological insufficiency of the world, which in turn drives him back to the ultimacy of a transcendent First Cause. Man's innate sense of wonder is divinely implanted. The ultimate beatitude of man is in the operation of his intellect, which will not rest until it reaches the source of its being. "Hence it must be granted absolutely that the blessed see the essence of God."[15] Less extreme than Maimonides, Aquinas will not agree that nonrational creatures escape the care of divine providence. Yet for Thomas too, providence resides in the intellect, and God is "the cause of things by His intellect."[16]

The Therapeutic of Knowledge

To suffer ignorance is to experience the wrath of God. Ignorance is separation from God. Pascal, cited earlier as bemoaning the ludicrous lot of the "thinking reed" cast into the endless night of the universe, finds comfort in the dignity of knowing. But if the universe were to crush him, man would still be more noble than that which killed him, because he knows that he dies and the advantage which the universe has over him, but the universe knows nothing of this.[17]

Metaphysical theodicies, we will later observe, generally find consolation less in the promise to transform the affliction than in the awareness of the ways of the universe. As Job concedes in the epilogue, ignorance is the despair which ends in sin: "Therefore have I uttered that which I understood not." Conversely, wisdom is the therapy which binds whole the broken spirit. "I know that Thou canst do everything, and that no purpose can be withheld from Thee."[18] Knowledge may be impotent in altering his lot, but knowledge of the metaphysical God who binds the chains of the Pleiades and looses the bonds of Orion relieves him of the dread of ignorance.

Even within a Spinozistic universe devoid of potentialities, the prophetic power of the intellect may free man from puerile resentments born of small vision. *Sub specie aeternitatis,* under the aspect of eternity, nothing need be hated. Affliction need not turn us against God. "Therefore, insofar as we understand God to be the cause of pain, we to that extent feel pleasure."[19] Neither to cry nor to laugh, only to understand. The drive to know seeks stability. It will not rest until it apprehends that ideally perfect being in whose omniscience the cause and telos of the universe resides. Therein lies a major motive of metaphysical theodicy. Such an intellectual soteriology is not limited to the age of Aquinas. A contemporary version of such a religious-metaphysical position is articulated in Michael Novak's fidelity to the drive to understand. Intellectual passion serves him as the keystone of human salvation. To contribute toward the "merging intelligibility of a world process" is a moral and creative *imitatio dei.*[20] For him, as for his mentor, B.J.F. Lonergan, God is the radical why behind the drive to understand, the source of understanding and of intelligibility in man.

The root metaphor of the drive to know is optical. The goal is *visio intellectualis,* to see God, to share the sweep of His vision under the aspect of eternity. The mind's eye leaps from effect to cause, from contingency to necessity, from the finite to the infinite, from the moving to the unmoved, from the relative to the absolute, until one beholds the Cause of all causes and the End of all ends. The God which the cognitive drive seeks is ideally a God who knows perfectly, and whose knowledge acts to will an intelligible order.

In the classic metaphysical tradition, such a God is marked by ultimate self-sufficiency and self-consciousness. Awareness of self is all that is necessary for awareness of others. The perfection of God's thinking, according to the Aristotelian paragon, is "in being superior to thinking of aught besides himself. The reason is that with us welfare involves a something beyond us, but the deity is his own well-being."[21] Those motivated by the drive to know find solace in a self-sufficient Absolute Intellect. For them, the immutability of perfect intelligence would be flawed by attention to changeable creatures, and the impassibility of a perfectly impartial intelligence would be compromised by attention to changeable creatures. Allowing God to be subject to the wants and needs of others would flaw the impassibility of a perfectly impartial intelligence. The logic of the drive to know yields an ideal omniscience which neither needs nor desires company. The introverted wisdom of an Aristotelian God, adopted by the classic tradition of metaphysical theology, remains a self-sufficient "thinking about thinking" (*noesia noesos noesia*).[22]

The rationalistic knowledge of God is restricted to that information mediated by observation of nature, by deductions from effect to cause, by inferences from consequences to logical ground. Such a metaphysical orientation expresses a formal relationship between God and His creation, a relationship in terms of power. But such an approach proscribes any penetration into the intent and motivation of God's activity. A limit is placed upon deductions of God's nature from observation of natural effects. As Maimonides contends, it would be logically illicit to ascribe anger or wrath or justice to God from observation of events such as hurricanes, earthquakes, mountains, and seas. From such phenomena one can at best argue for His power, for His metaphysical attributes but not for His moral attributes. For benevolent, wicked, or indifferent gods may all produce identical effects.

The actions ascribed to God may be similar to human actions which originate in identifiable psychological dispositions; but logic properly denies the right to ascribe such dispositions to the divine causative agent on analogical grounds. Consequently, the logic of the cognitive drive tends to favor ascription of metaphysical over moral attributes of God. The tendency to overlay the attributes of benevolence and justice with a metaphysical construction is critical for metaphysical theodicies. Such rationalistic predilections are not likely to yield a God-idea with emphasis on personalistic or moral attributes. "All we understand is the fact that He exists, that He is a being to whom none of His creatures is similar, who has nothing in common with them."[23] In this extreme Maimonidean formulation, no correlation between God and any of His creatures is allowed. We will show that the less rigid Thomistic position, for all its use of analogical predication, yields little more information as to the personal and moral traits of God than Maimonides' negative theology. The difference between God and man is not simply one of degree but admits of no true comparison whatever. The drive to know is content with a self-sufficient, omniscient, and omnipotent being. It fails to satisfy the drive to be known, whose needs call for another way of knowing and another relationship between God and man.

The Drive to Be Known

Aristotle is said to have declared that man's thought of God springs from two sources -- the experience of the soul and the phenomenon of heaven. If the drive to know attaches itself to the phenomenon of heaven and is revealed in the rhythmic order of celestial orbits, the drive to be known is derived from the experience of the soul. The basic drive is not toward cognition but toward recognition; not to know as much as to be known; not knowledge but acknowledgment of a concerned deity. What excites the adoration of the psalmist is that in the vastness of the universe, the maker of the heavens and earth is mindful of man and cares for the son of man, making him but little less than God and crowning him with honor and glory (Psalm 8). It is not the fear of ignorance but the dread of being ignored which oppresses man. Not the mystery of the invisible God but the muteness of the impersonal God leads to human despair.

Judah Halevi, writing in the eleventh century, expressed this religious quest for recognition, which he found in the God of the prophets as contrasted with the God of the philosophers. The latter describe *Elohim*, the deity apprehended by metaphysical speculation. The philosophers are caught up in "the desire to demonstrate." But the benefit of such cognitive desire is to be found "only in the cognizance of the true nature of things, in order to resemble the Active Intellect."[24] The philosopher's axiom is that of the evil men admonished by the prophet Zephaniah. "The Lord will not do good nor will He do evil." Such a God with all His cognitive perfection "neither benefits nor injures, and knows nothing of our prayers, offerings, obedience or disobedience."[25] By contrast, the God of the prophets is responsive to the human drive to be known and will not be pacified by knowledge of an impersonally ordered universe.

Buber's critique of the philosophic orientation of religion echoes Halevi's. The "noetical act" which ends with "knowledge of an object which is indifferent to being known" is wholly in error. The knowledge which faith brings relates to "an undemonstrable and unprovable" being who is nevertheless known as caring and as one from whom all meaning derives.[26]

If, as we have said, the critical metaphor of the drive to know is optical, the crucial metaphor of the drive to be known is auditory. The goal is to hear God, to know oneself to be called by Him who listens and responds. The saddest proposition of religious philosophy is the Epicurean formulation of gods who exist and know but who do not care and do not intervene.

So, for the drive to be known, the analogical link which unites man and God is not intellect but personality. The relationship between man and God is not of a metaphysical order based upon the structural similarity between cause and effect, but of an existential order based on the kinship of personalities. Thus the knowledge of God is experienced as immediate because it originates out of inner acquaintance and is not mediated by rational demonstration. The acquaintance is natural in that it comes much the way man discovers himself. "He discovers something that is identical with himself although it transcends him infinitely, something from which he is estranged, but from which he never has been and never can be separated."[27]

By contrast to the active rational quest for knowledge of God, the quest for recognition strikes one as far more passive. The type of knowledge relationship which satisfies the drive to be known is expressed in Buber's awareness that "my limited knowledge opens out into a state in which I am boundlessly known" by a comprehending Thou.[28] Karl Barth's true witness similarly typifies a receptive knowing which is appropriate to the relationship between God and man. Acknowledgment of God characterizes this knowing relationship. It is a knowledge born of faith and demonstrated by trust in a divine personality whose will is veiled. God is acknowledged as "the one who knows him through and through."[29] Man knows God only insofar as he is known by God. Unlike the active element in the drive to know, which flows from some innate disposition in man, the drive to be known admits of no such natural capacity grounded in man. Man hopes and waits to be addressed. Something must happen to him. For, in the biblical context, truth is not possessed but experienced as "personal fellowship."[30]

Additionally, the truth gained in the encounter of persons, unlike that of metaphysically oriented theology, cannot be claimed as something static and timeless. The acknowledged God of recognition is other than that directed by the cognitive drive. As Charles McCoy puts it in describing the theology derived from biblical faith, "One does not so much know God in the philosophical sense as one is possessed by God and known by him in an intensely personal sense."[31] Theology in the biblical view is a recital of God's acts, not of man's philosophical discourses. Not His ontological immutability but His steadfastness, not His omniscience but His relatedness, not His impassibility but His responsiveness, not His transcendence but His involvement are experienced. It is the acknowledgment that we are known which the drive for recognition celebrates. The bilateral relationship sought by the drive to be known spawns a personalistic vocabulary of "judgment," "forgiveness," "redemption," "responsibility," and "loyalty." Here the analogy in the knowing-acknowledging relationship with God is in the encounter between human beings. Granted the transcendent distance between the personalities, the language resulting from the drive to be known is inescapably anthropomorphic.

To sum up, the polar aspirations we have identified do not proceed blindly. Each appetite seeks out its end through some envisaged fulfillment of its craving. In much the same sense that the questioner is said to know beforehand the kind of answer which is acceptable to his query, the believer knows the kind of being which alone will satisfy his religious quest. In Aquinas's idiom, "everything seeks after its own perfection, and the perfection and form of an effect consists in a certain likeness to the agent since every agent makes its like."[32]

The drive to know aspires toward its cognitive ideal, toward being who preeminently knows. Whatever other traits such a being may possess, they are qualified and ordered to complement the essential attribute of perfect knowledge. The drive to be known is drawn toward a personal figure whose major attributes express His cognizance and interest in His creation, man in particular. Each drive then prefigures a distinctive idea of perfection, which shapes its own concept of God. We may draw upon the Thomistic formulation: "All things, by desiring their own perfection, desire God Himself, inasmuch as the perfection of all things are so many similitudes of the divine being."[33] Thomas's metaphysical account has its counterpart in Feuerbach's psychological version. "What is finite to the understanding," Feuerbach wrote, "is nothing to the heart."[34] The heart of the drives extends its imagination toward infinity, toward an objective and independent perfect being. Each of the drives favors its own epistemology, anticipates a unique relationship between man and God, and culminates in its particular idea of divine perfection. Each notion of divine perfection in turn fashions its own theodicy.

Chapter 2
The Idea of Perfection: The Core Presupposition of Theodicy

The perfections of God are those of our souls, but He possesses them in boundless measure.

--Leibniz

Professor Stephen Toulmin, in his inquiry into the aims and evolution of science, points to the "ideals of natural order," which have for the scientist something self-evident and absolute about them like the "basic presuppositions" of which R.G. Collingwood wrote.[1] These ideals, or paradigms, are neither naively true nor naively false; they are more or less fruitful in their explanatory powers. Depending on the particular paradigm held, certain phenomena may strike one scientist as highly unexpected and another as perfectly natural. The former had certain prior expectations which "made" the event unexpected.[2] The replacement of one ideal by another, Toulmin demonstrated, is critical to the understanding of the profound changes in scientific understanding and foresight. "There must always be some point in a scientist's explanation where he comes to a stop: beyond this point, if he is pressed to explain further the fundamental basis of his explanation, he can say only that he has reached rock bottom."[3]

Theologians similarly function with basic, self-evident paradigms in their conceptualization of God, and their understanding of His relationship to the universe. These paradigms are equally neither true nor false, but they are essential to the framing of the question, to the identification of the problem, and to its solution. The core paradigm of theology and the one which looms large in dictating the kind of theodicy to be employed is the idea of perfection. What is anticipated about the ways of God and

His relationship to creation depends largely upon the particular idea of divine perfection tacitly held by the theologian.

The presuppositions of perfection which are believed in cultivate a whole set of expectations concerning the character of the universe and the proper conduct of its divine governor. They prepare the way for experiencing and interpreting events. Which event is evil and why it may be allowed by God depends upon the particular notion of divine perfection held. Prior to his experienced afflictions, Job is already committed to a specific idea of divine perfection without which his entire problematic could not have arisen. Antecedent ideals have led him to anticipate a state of affairs appropriate to God's conduct and relationship to man. Only on the basis of those expectations do Job's sufferings appear inexplicable; only on the grounds of some specific perfection ideal are the explanations of Job's friends rendered intelligible. The perfection ideal contains cognitive and affective values which are simply taken for granted.

As in the case of the scientist's ideal order of nature, the theologian's perfection ideal functions on a half-conscious level in selecting and ordering the hierarchy of attributes ascribable to the supreme being. The perfection paradigm is implicitly appealed to in arguments calling for theological justification. An understanding of the governing role of the perfection image is particularly important to bear in mind inasmuch as the identification and explanation of evil in theodicy depends upon the controlling logic of the perfection paradigm.

Before characterizing the influence of the preconceptual idea of perfection upon theologies and their theodicies, we would caution against possible misunderstanding of our approach. While cultural and psychological factors clearly play a crucial role in forming ideas of divine perfection, questions of their origin and ontological independence are not our concern. We mean to "bracket" all ontological interpretations of the perfection idea.
Ideals are not born de novo. But their origin in no way attests to their truth or ontological status. Etiology is not ontology.
The psycho-sociogenic sources of our perfection ideals are logically irrelevant in judging their validity and truth. The con-

fusion of origins with grounds, we suspect, may explain the neglect by theological analysis of the critical role of the perfection paradigm in shaping theological systems. Suspicion of what the Roman Catholic Church in 1861 officially condemned as "ontologism" may have discouraged theologians from examining this major a priori category of theological discourse.[4] To avoid dealing with the presuppositional character of the perfection ideal on such grounds would be to succumb to the genetic fallacy.

Perfection Models in Theology

Whether God exists or not is the last question to be asked, though it is the fashion of many theologians to make it the first question. Before men can speak meaningfully of God or seek to demonstrate His existence, they must know what it is they are looking for. They must know beforehand where they are to look for corroborative evidence and what would count as confirming proofs of His existence and attributes. They must know beforehand which events and traits point to His reality, which features in the real or ideal world may be legitimately used to draw analogies of God's nature, which claims to revelation may be said to be His self-disclosures, which actions may be asserted to belong to His will.

Martin Buber, for example, insists that "nothing can make me believe in a God who punishes Saul because he did not murder his enemy."[5] "Nothing" presumably means that no biblical text or second revelation or rational argument can alter his invincible conviction concerning God's conduct. Clearly, however, Saul's punishment by God contradicts no logical or metaphysical law. What is this apodictic certainty on Buber's part but an indication of his fidelity to an antecedent commitment, to an idea of divine perfection whose logic precludes God's acting in certain ways? Indeed, Buber goes on to explain that there is nothing astonishing in the fact that an observant Jew, "when he has to choose between God and the Bible, chooses God: The God in whom he believes, Him in whom he can believe."[6] The logic of "can" in this argument makes oblique reference to an unexamined but imperious idea of divine perfection. However unformulated, the image of perfection contains implicit criteria as to what may or may not be properly attributed to God.

The Abraham of the Scriptures similarly insists that a contemplated destruction of innocents along with the guilty is "far from" the character of the covenant God. And, in a passage in his *Streit der Fakultäten*, Kant would have Abraham answer the voice commanding his sacrifice of Isaac in a similar fashion: "That I ought not to kill my son is certain beyond a shadow of a doubt; that you, as you appear to be, are God, I am not convinced and will never be even if your voice resounded from heaven." The positive and negative convictions Kant expresses are rooted in a faith commitment to a particular idea of divine perfection. Fidelity to a similar typology of divine perfection finds expression in John Stuart Mill's declaration:

> Whatever power such a being [God] may have over me, there is one thing he shall not do. He shall not compel me to worship him. I will call no being good, who is not what I mean when I apply that epithet to my fellow creature, and if such a being can sentence me to hell for not so calling him, to hell I will go.[7]

More than semantic lucidity is involved in Mill's outburst. He "cannot" worship amoral omnipotence because it runs counter to an ultimate commitment to his ideal of perfection. That neither Kierkegaard nor Karl Barth would respond in this fashion points to their significantly different presuppositions of divine perfection.

Theologians "know" that God cannot square a circle or cannot create a moral being devoid of free will or create a world without some evil. They argue as if the issue were a matter of objective logic alone. Beneath the manifest logical argumentation, however, resides a latent perfection ideal with its own legislative logic as to the powers and conduct of a supremely perfect being. Theological limitations upon the attributes of "omniscience," "omnipotence," "benevolence" may be traced to the prescriptions of the particular perfection model to which the theologian is antecedently committed. Thus, Aristotle knows how the gods will behave and what they must do. "Will not gods seem absurd if they make contracts and return deposits, and so on?"[8] Aristotle's tacit appeal to his idea of perfection allows him to assert confidently that gods will not be assigned acts of justice or bravery or liberality or moderation since they are "unworthy of gods." The logic of his idea of perfection centered around the ideal of self-sufficiency leads him to conclude: "Therefore, the activity of God, which surpasses all others in blessedness, must be contemplative."[9] On the basis of another ideal of divine perfection, the Bible finds God's keeping of contracts, pledges, oaths, and covenants far from seeming absurd.

The Tacit Dimension of the Perfection Idea

Whatever logical limitations Anselm's arguments for the existence of God may betray, his ontological approach is highly suggestive for theological analysis. Antecedent to his proof of existence is his reliance upon a pre-philosophic belief in perfection. His prayer in the second chapter of the *Proslogion* calls for a demonstration after the fact of faith in perfection. He prays that he be given to understand that God is that which he believes. Even the obdurate fool must see that "something exists, in the understanding, at least, than which nothing greater can be thought."[10] Theologians may argue as to what properties belong to the ideal of "the greatest," but even here they are guided by commitment to some idea of perfection. Thus, the finitist theologian limits God's omnipotence so as to preserve what for him is the essential mark of divine perfection, i.e., the goodness of God.

The image of divine perfection in theology resembles the normative ideal, except that the former claims to generate its own existence. The perfection model, moreover, determines the reality of other attributes ascribed to it. This may explain the theologian's use of imperatives when arguing what God can or cannot, must or must not, be or do. The presupposition of perfection requires no proof of its reality because the ideal itself determines what is real. Reality does not announce itself. An antecedent ideal presents the criteria which judge what is real and what is illusory. Anselm's ontological way brings to the surface the hidden logic of the perfection ideal in theology generally. The self-evident character of the idea of perfection "proves" God's existence. For many, the apparent weakness of the ontological argument suggests Harry Wolfson's explanation that we are dealing with a "psychological" and not an "ontological" argument. For Anselm, Descartes, and Spinoza, the reality of the idea of perfection requires no proof because it carries with it the certitude of immediate knowledge. As Wolfson concludes, "The reality of the idea of God was never sought to be proven by the syllogism, but was conceived to be established in the same way that the reality of anything is immediately perceived and experienced."[11]

We would, however, explain this psychological certainty of the three philosophers cited as derived from their commonly held faith in a perfection ideal. The reality of God is "immediately known" because the ideality believed in is presupposed. Given a different idea of perfection the necessary entailment of existence as a predicate of God may not follow so surely. For a Hindu or a Buddhist, it is far from "manifest by the natural light" that that which exists outside the understanding is "greater" or "better" than that which exists in the understanding alone, or whether existence itself is part of perfection.

While every theology is informed by an idea of divine perfection, not all ideas of divine perfection are alike. Maimonides, for example, was convinced that the perfection of God was an "innate idea."[12] He was equally convinced that everyone shared his idea of perfection. Such an assumption of the universality of what proves to be a particular notion of perfection is not unique to Maimonides. As a prereflective presupposition, the idea of perfection frequently functions in theological argumentation as if its image were self-evident. In this presumption lies the concealed root of some major theological entanglements. Theologians formulating their theodicies do not feel compelled to justify the unique character of their perfection paradigm. They proceed to mount arguments against adversaries without feeling the need to justify their taken-for-granted presuppositions of infinite perfection. Nor, for that matter, do they sense the need to contend with the perfection ideals that support the adversaries' posture.

The perfection model of classical metaphysical theology is significantly different from the models that support process, existentialist, or personalistic theological orientations. Each perfection typology marks the scope of its theological domain and weights the qualities it assigns to God differently, and all without explicit, cognitive awareness. The presuppositional character of the perfection ideal, which unconsciously colors our theological conceptualizations, tends to blind us from seeing the pluralism of these ideals in theology and the profound effect they have upon theological justification.

The physicist Eddington offers the parable of a man studying deep-sea life by means of casting nets of a two-inch-thick mesh into the waters. The man concludes that there are no fish smaller than two inches in the sea. Each theology throws out its own size-category of perfection. It may indeed be a necessary instrument for the theological enterprise. But it would be an error to presume on that account that there is but one such size. It may prove a liberating knowledge to understand that every doctrine of God's perfection depends upon certain unarguable, accepted ideals, whatever their source.

Perfection as a Principle of Vindication

Uncovering the dwelt-in ideas of divine perfection is particularly illuminating for understanding the depth arguments of theodicies. The perfection paradigms of theology are not readily in evidence because they are rarely recognized for what they are. The ideal is not the focal object of the theologian. It is tacitly accepted and used in doing theology. The presuppositions of the perfection ideal underlying a given theology may be deduced from the explicit arguments used by the theologian. The theologian, like the scientist, may not notice the paradigmatic lens through which he perceives the situation. "There is only one way of seeing one's spectacles clearly; that is, to take them off. It is impossible to focus both on them and through them at the same time."[13] The unique character of the perfection ideal is thus largely hidden from the theologian. Its very obviousness enables its concealment. The perfection model is the assumed premise, not the argued conclusion of theological demonstrations. Everything is seen in the light, but the light is not noticed.

The perfection idea, then, functions within a theological system much as a paradigm functions in a language game. To use one of Wittgenstein's illustrations, one cannot rightly ask what the length of the standard meter in Paris is in the manner that we may ask about the length of some piece of metal. For by convention, "length" means being measured against the standard meter in Paris.[14] Analogously, the perfection idea serves theology as a paradigm measuring the qualities and attributes ascribed to the Perfect Being according to its own standards.

The perfection idea in theology may be understood as an ultimate conviction precisely in the sense that Polanyi characterizes it.

> We can voice our ultimate convictions only from within our convictions, from within the whole system of acceptances that are logically prior to any particular assertion of our own, prior to the holding of any particular piece of knowledge.[15]

The governing image of perfection generates a network of commitment which sustains and protects it. The insular and internal character of the perfection ideal within a theological system renders it virtually invulnerable to external criticism. The perfection ideal is self-validating. We are thus enveloped in what Charles McCoy calls "the theological predicament." In dealing with ultimate commitments of faith, "one is concerned with the source of all criteria of truth and error, good and evil. One cannot validate a realm of actuality by criteria beyond it."[16]

What rational justification can be demanded of ultimate

convictions in a perfection ideal? We suggest that they are no more subject to *justificanda cognitiones* than are the laws of logic or the principle of the uniformity of nature. We can, at best, turn to Herbert Feigl's proposal that the latter "laws" can be defended as *justificanda actionis*.[17] Applied to the faith presuppositions of ideas of perfection, we may offer pragmatic vindication of our ideals. Perfection-ideas may be vindicated as indispensable instruments of theological conceptualization much as the laws of logic are justified as pragmatically necessary for rational communication. Beyond that, perfection ideas may be vindicated in terms of their ability to satisfy the basic needs and interests of the believer, e.g., his drive to know and his drive to be known. On such grounds, ideals of perfection may be appraised as better or worse, not true or false.

The insular character of theology which the ultimate commitments and absolute presuppositions assure may be cracked only "from within the whole system of acceptances." The crisis of evil touches off an internal strife among the discovered multiplicity of perfection ideals inherent in monotheism. It is not the multiplicity of ideals but their incompatibility which penetrates the solidity of our ultimate commitments. The crises of evil challenge the assumption that one single idea of perfection or group of perfection ideas held together simultaneously can satisfy the various needs of the religious man. From this viewpoint of theological analysis, theodicy may be seen as the clarification or refinement of the major ideal of perfection to which it owes allegiance.

Thomas's Five Ways

The subterranean control of the idea of perfection in formulating theological positions which we have proposed may be illustrated by examining Aquinas's classic proofs for the existence of God. The set of assumptions lodged in his perfection ideal and his proofs are taken for granted. They are presumptions so much a part of the climate of opinion that they need not be argued. The conclusion of each of the proofs appeals to a popular consensus to confirm the identification of his metaphysical conclusions with the name of God. Having arrived at a first efficient cause or an unmoved mover, Thomas typically concludes, "and this everyone understands to be God," or "this all men speak of as God," or "to which everyone gives the name of God."[18] Thomas here appeals to the common usage of his day. But that connection of first, efficient, and final causes with the name of God and not with the name of nature or the Form of Good or the names of gods carries more freight than the ordinary language of the day. In it is embedded the implicit cultural ideals within his theological circle. "All men," "everyone" insinuates universality without argument. Clearly, listeners committed to personalistic or process theologies and their idealities would not so readily acquiesce to the identification of necessitarian and immutable qualities with the true marks of God. Not only do the arguments of his proofs turn upon acceptance of a particular idea of perfection but the idea is presupposed to be universally held.

The first three ways of Thomas depend upon a number of assumptions entailed in his idea of divine perfection: That the existence of changeable things requires an explanation in terms of being not changeable itself; that an explanation is incomplete until it is grounded in a causeless cause; that actuality is prior to possibility in fact and in value; that there must be a sufficient reason to account for the existence of a contingent world. These arguments appear self-evident only to those who are committed a priori to a particular metaphysically determined image of perfection. The ontological insufficiency of the universe Aquinas senses is experienced only by those whose antecedent perfection ideals share similar expectations and standards.

Turning to the proofs themselves, the fifth way barely conceals the unargued image of perfection governing the argument. Here he appeals to our common observation that even those things which lack knowledge "act for an end, and this is evident from their acting always, or nearly always, in the same way, so as to obtain the best result."[19] Things without consciousness, Thomas concludes, can reach such benevolent purpose only by the direction of an intelligent being. Aquinas, of course, simply assumes a preconceived notion as to what constitutes the "best" purpose for such things as physical bodies. The teleological ideal, critical to this argument, points to an unproven and unprovable expression of an Aristotelian rationalistic idea of perfection.

The argument in the fourth way appeals to the manner in which things are graded "more" or "less" according as they approach the standard of "the most." We are thus led to the odd conclusion that "there is something which is truest, something best, something noblest and, consequently, something which is most being, for those things that are greatest in truth are greatest in being."[20] It would appear that the argument is but another version of Anselm's ontological proof, which Thomas had earlier refuted.[21] The need to step from comparative degrees to an absolute is questionable; but the leap from an idea of "the most" to its reification seems to echo the fallacy in the ontological argument. This is more evidently the case when Aquinas, in the same argument, transforms the normative idea of "the most" into a causative agency. "Now the maximum in any genus is the cause of all in that genus, as fire, which is the maximum of heat, is the cause of all hot things."[22] Here the highest and most-valued stage is turned into an originating cause. Aquinas concludes his argument: "Therefore there *must* also be something which is to all beings the *cause* of their being, goodness, and every other *perfection*: and this we call God."[23] All excellences are thus united and lodged in an idea of perfection which must exist.

To the question "What is God?" and to the question "Is there a God?" the answer is one and the same, Aquinas argues. Consequently, "to those seeing the divine essence in itself, it is supremely self-evident that God exists because his essence is his being."[24] Our interest is not simply to note the parallel to the ontological argument which underlies Aquinas's proofs, an observation made by Kant, but to illustrate in a major theological intellect the ubiquitous role of perfection, which selects the attributes it ascribes to God and may even generate His existence.

It is in Aquinas's use of analogical reasoning that the dominant role of perfection appears most conspicuous. Analogical vision does not operate like the disinterested eye of the camera.

It will not view all creaturely qualities as equally eligible for ascription to God. Aquinas, moreover, is not willing to settle for Maimonides' strictures against attribution, limiting them to negative attributes alone. For Thomas such positive affirmations of God's wisdom and goodness signify more than negations. "For in saying that God lives, they [who speak of God] assuredly mean more than to say that He is the cause of our life, or that He differs from inanimate bodies."[25] If so, by what criteria are selections of attributes drawn from the natural realm to be applied to God? Wherein does he deem moral and intellectual virtues to be analogically appropriate to God but not affective and corporeal traits? The criteria and justification are self-evident only to those who share an Aristotelian-Thomistic idea of metaphysical perfection. Mormon theology and certain mystic theologies have found no difficulty in assigning physical form to God.

Beyond the analogy of direct attribution, Thomistic theology employs an analogy of proportionality to further qualify the perfections attributable to God. A proper ratio between the natural and supernatural orders is called for in order to appropriately assign qualities from one realm to another. Care is to be taken to consider the separate nature of the analogates. Perfections flowing from God to creatures exist in a higher state in God himself. Whenever a name taken from any created perfection is attributed to God, there must be separated from its signification anything that belongs to the imperfect mode proper to creatures.

> As regards what is signified by these names, they belong properly to God, and more properly than they belong to creatures, and are applied primarily to Him. But as regards their mode of signification, they do not properly and strictly apply to God; for their mode of signification befits creatures.[26]

But by what criteria are we to separate that character which belongs to imperfection without our knowing the nature of the higher state in God? If the positive attributes, the "pure perfections," such as wisdom and goodness, preexist in God in a supereminent and infinite degree, in what sense do they convey information of their character other than in the sense of the negative attributes? Does not judgment of the mode of signification as well as direct attribution presuppose a tacit perfection ideal? How can the analogy of proportionality operate without some assumptions as to the nature of the supernatural analogate, and do these in turn not depend upon unproven and unprovable a priori notions of perfection? In what sense can it be said, for example, that "God loves"? Is divine love, drawn analogically from the natural order in which human love is experienced, subject to frustations, affected by the acceptance or rejection of others, initiated by God or responsive to human adoration? Whatever answers may be given to such questions will depend upon the type of prerational ideal of perfection held by the theologian. The character of the ideal will prescribe the nature of the divine analogate, though it may be articulated in a descriptive mode. The decision as to whether pain and suffering are to be ascribed to God is dependent upon a perfection paradigm which judges the propriety of such ascription. The logic of analogy does not proceed presuppositionless. Its selective perception is guided by an act of aspiration.

The idea of divihe perfection is a multifunctional regulative ideal. To use Kant's terminology, it yields synthetic a priori judgments in theology. For it establishes necessary connections between the subject and its predicates; at the same time, the subject it describes is independent of experience and cannot be refuted by observation. And like Kant's characterization of synthetic a priori knowledge, the theological claims which derive from the perfection ideal carry with them the conviction of necessity and universality. It is an a priori of experience and valuation, a hidden theological monitor, which reigns unchallenged except when its foundation is shaken from within.

Chapter 3

The Single Mind of Metaphysical Theodicy

Will ye reply: "You do but illustrate
the iron laws that chain the will of God"?

Did fallen Lisbon deeper drink of vice
Than London, Paris, or sunlit Madrid?

"All's well," ye say, "and all is necessary."
Think ye this universe had been the worse
Without this hellish gulf in Portugal?

God I respect, yet love the universe.
Not pride, alas, it is, but love of man,
To mourn so terrible a stroke as this.

. . . and as, with quaking voice,
Mortal and pitiful, ye cry, "All's well,"
The universe belies you, and your heart
Refutes a hundred times your mind's conceit.

--Voltaire, "Poem on the Lisbon Disaster"

We turn now to a major strand of divine perfection in Western monotheism out of which the central arguments of metaphysical theodicy are woven. The constellation of attributes which describe the God idea are not arbitrarily thrown together. Invariably a fixed star, a major predicate of divinity, magnetizes the satellite attributes. They gravitate around the luminary center and reflect its light.

The fixed center of the classic metaphysical ideal of perfection is the attribute of understanding or wisdom. It is the dominant attribute sought by the drive to know. The other attributes stand as variables to this constant. Omnipotence, will, goodness are all accordingly limited by the ideal of omniscience. The auxiliary attributes are not allowed to compromise the infinite wisdom of God. Omnipotence will be allowed its reign but not when it threatens to violate the laws of logic. The rationalistic ideal will not countenance the power to break the laws of identity, contradiction, and the excluded middle. "There can be no will of God regarding those things which are inherently impossible."[1] As the major legislating predicate, reason sets limits upon the will. God is free but He cannot will that which the understanding knows to be absurd. Such a will is a slave to passions. For the intellectual ideal, then, will and intellect are one and the same thing.[2] Even in His miraculous activity, such a deity acts within the bounds of reason. The cognitive ideal allows Leibniz to state with full confidence that the will of God is not independent of the rules of wisdom.

Ludwig Feuerbach observed that the divine being of "theology" is the being of intellect, and offered as evidence the fact that the attributes of God are not determinations of sensation or imagination but those of reason. The "ontotheological predicates" are merely predicates of the understanding.[3] The ultimate presupposition of metaphysical theology sets understanding as the highest and noblest mark of perfect being. It is, therefore, not altogether surprising that the traits of ideal knowledge coincide with the attributes of God. Whatever reason requires for its realization is ascribed to God's perfection. Classical theology engages in an *imitatio rationis*. As reason is immaterial, God is imageless; as the intellect transcends the bribes of passion, God is impassible; as truth is not limited by space or time, God is eternal and transcendent; as reason exercises its faculty impartially, God's general providence is distributed justly to all; as perfect wisdom envelops all that is or will be, God is omnipresent; as perfect knowledge requires an object to be known, God is creator of His world; as reason is qualitatively infinite, God is infinite power; as reason judges, God is judge; as knowledge is the principle of action, God acts in knowing; as truth is indivisible, unchangeable, and necessary, so is God simple, immutable, and absolute; as knowledge is objective and independent, so God is not subject to control.

Two Ideals of Perfect Knowledge

We have spoken of the cognitive ideal as if it were of one piece. Clearly not all ideals of knowledge are uniform, and different epistemological ideals will accordingly alter the status, range, and interrelationships of the theological attributes. Theologians committed to an Aristotelian ideal of omniscience, for example, judge God's relationship to contingency, potentiality, change, and time differently from the theologians we will examine in the next chapter, who have adopted a cognitive ideal derived from process philosophy.

For the former (e.g., Maimonides, Aquinas), God's wisdom is measured by eternity. He knows at once, in the eternal present, all that is or will be. For Him, there is no successive, cumulative knowledge. Reason is the same for all eternity, since knowledge, which is perfect, does not increase as the future unfolds. God's omnivorous intellect extends "over all time, and to all things which exist in any time, as objects present to Him."[4] Perfect knowledge is time-transcending, devoid of any temporal condition. Divine knowledge is not subject to change. The proper object of such a knowledge ideal is similarly untouched by change. Infinite intelligence insists that the world to be known should be invested with commensurate metaphysical dignity lest intelligence be contaminated by the object of contemplation. For knowledge is a communion. In the Aristotelian formulation, "Since, then, thought and the object of thought are not different in the case of things that have not matter, the divine thought and its object will be the same, i.e., the thinking will be one with the object of its thought."[5] Here we note again the generative character of the rational ideal, which creates an environment suitable to its nature. Knowledge, which is unsurpassable, calls for a universe of form devoid of change-infected matter, a universe so structured that it can be known through the categories of universality, necessity, and actuality. "According to the mode of immateriality is the mode of cognition."[6]

Out of much the same intellectualistic tradition, Maimonides removed God from all relation to time. Time is an accident connected with motion, and motion is a condition to which only material bodies are subject, while God is immaterial.[7] God cannot be surprised by the future. There is no novelty under the sun, no contingency or change which God may discover later. Perfect knowledge knows no degrees; it does not change, for if it did, it would not be as perfect as before. A changeless divine intellect will not respond to the need of others, for to respond is to admit to change and thus to contradict the immutability and self-sufficiency of Ideal Intellect.

To the theologian for whom the Aristotelian ideal prevails, God's knowledge and life are one; the subject, object, and action of knowledge are identical. "The intellectus, the intelligens and the intelligible are in God one and the same thing."[8] As God thinketh, so is the universe and so His attributes.

Where the ideal of perfect knowledge differs, the character of the divine attributes is altered. In the world of process philosophy, growth, novelty, and responsiveness to change are identified as the traits of exemplary knowledge. The receptive capaciousness of knowledge is valued over the possession of knowledge. Discursive knowledge, the traditional mark of imperfect wisdom, is celebrated as the sign of a limitlessly growing intelligence. When a future event comes to fruition, the process philosopher Charles Hartshorne affirms, an omniscient mind will know more than it did before. It will know all that there is. True knowledge corresponds to reality. The future, which has not happened, is not real. To know that which is not real is to know falsely. The future is indeterminate and not subject to true knowledge.[9] The new ideal of omniscience, saturated with the evolutionary spirit, challenges the older ideal of permanent and complete knowledge.

The cumulative intelligence of the divine mind is the truest virtue of the ideal knower. That God can and will know more than He now knows testifies to the excellence of His cognitive capacity. No epistemological embarrassment follows from the admission that perfect intelligence does not know the future. It points to the reality and openness of the future. Not knowing the future is no failure of God's unsurpassable knowledge. On the contrary, to know the future now is to know what is not, and thus to know falsely. Given this nonclassical cognitive ideal, it appears contradictory for God to know as actual that which is potential. Given this notion of evolving intellect, omniscience is temporalized and the perfect being assumes a different and positive relationship to time, contingency, mutability, futurity, and potentiality. A deity whose virtue lies in His openness to the future will not be bound by the static character of traditional omniprescience, which has weighed so heavily against human freedom. Nor will divine intelligence, responsive to a dynamic universe, be considered demeaned by change and responsiveness to the suffering creation. The active-passive, giving-receiving, absolute-relative dipolar characterization of omniscience conceives of the perfect God as possessing the best of all compossible attributes. What are virtues in this concept of intelligence are scandalous imperfections for classic metaphysical theology. All depends upon the particular ideal of perfection and its body of assumptions to which the theologian, consciously or not, is committed. While the affinity between the classic and process metaphysical ideals of divine perfection is evident, particularly as they contrast with the biblical, personalistic ideals, there are sharp differences centering around the character ascribed to the attribute of understanding. These contrasts affect the kinds of arguments used in the classical and modern metaphysical theodicy.

Cognitive Perfection and the *Imitatio Dei*

The ideal of perfection, we have argued, serves to identify, coordinate and render compatible the attributes of God. It also serves as a model of life to be emulated by men. The paradigm of perfection pervades the value system of theology even as it forms the character of its divine being.

The classic theological cognitive ideal prescribes a gradation of human virtues, parallel to the hierarchical order of its divine attributes. In the concluding chapter of his *Guide of the Perplexed*, Maimonides lists four levels of human perfection in ascending order. He begins with the acquisition of material things, moves to the perfection of the body, and then to moral perfection. But, while moral perfection is the highest degree of excellence in man's character, it is not the true or final perfection of man. The acquisition of metaphysical knowledge is the true end, the highest perfection, the mark of man and the path to immortality.[10] Moral principles depend upon community. Yet, Maimonides urges his readers to consider man alone. In isolation from society, moral principles are superfluous; whereas contemplative wisdom is of supreme value and is sought for its own sake, even when divorced from community. Much as the introverted omniscience of his God needs no companionship, the true intellectual enjoys his relative self-sufficiency. Moral perfection is of instrumental value for achieving the environmental and personal tranquility requisite for deep intellectual communion with God. But moral conduct and even worship are yet subordinate to the *imitatio rationis*. Grace is given to man in knowing God and not to one "who merely fasts and prays."[11] Only the knowledge-seekers are permitted to draw near to Him. The ignorant incur His wrath; the knowers receive His favor.

In his discussion of man's ultimate happiness, Aquinas presents us with a hierarchy of human virtues similar to that of Maimonides' degrees of human perfection. External goods and goods of the body along with practical intellectual virtues and moral virtue are instrumentally valuable. Their value lies in their freeing man from wants and passions disturbing to man's proper end: the wisdom which is contemplation of divine things. Such contemplative operation makes man more self-sufficent and therein closer to God. The metaphysical cognitive ideal leads Aquinas to contrast the need for friends as an element of human happiness with "the perfect happiness which will be in our heavenly fatherland [where] the fellowship of friends is not essential to happiness" since men enjoy their perfection in God.[12] The attainment of perfect intellection is the highest aspiration of Thomas' man. For him, as for Maimonides, the active, moral, social life is important but auxiliary to the contemplative ideal.[13]

We have observed that the major ideal of divinity, wisdom, generates its own universe. The impulse to know bears a procreative impulse. For ideal knowledge is boundless and calls for an object adequate to its high standard; following one classic formulation, the fullness of all logically compossible things. Infinite knowledge spawns the notion of plenitude, the orderly variety and richness of being. The very excellence of infinite intelligence requires the creation of a suitably endowed universe. Wisdom, being, and goodness, the latter term understood in the metaphysical sense of fullness of being, are closely related. God in His wisdom and goodness is the supreme cause of all things. It is through His wisdom that He exercises His providential power. Inasmuch as God knows all things, all things may be said to come under His sovereignty.[14]

The arguments of certain rationalist theologians clearly exhibit the ontological generativeness of the cognitive ideal. A characteristic set of arguments, tightly presented by B. J. F. Lonergan, begins with the extrapolation from the properties of a restrictive act to those of an act of unrestricted understanding.[15] Since what is known by true understanding is being, and since the understanding knows itself, it follows that what is truly known must necessarily be. Moreover, perfect understanding is by definition self-explanatory, unconditional, independent, and invulnerable to correction or improvement. Further, an unrestricted act of understanding is self-reflective and thus understands itself as an intelligible being. Consequently, the object or primary being of perfect self-understanding must be as perfect as the understanding in order for it to grasp itself as unconditional. That primary being cannot exist contingently since the contingent is not self-explanatory and is thus incompatible with unrestricted understanding.

The primary being of such self-reflective perfect understanding, in order to qualify as its proper object, must itself be intelligent, independent, necessarily existent, unique, simple, timeless, actual, free, omnipotent -- in short, God. The necessity invoked here is that of a logical order and flows from the premises of intellectual perfection.

Wisdom, in its ideal formulation, plays a restrictive as well as a generative role in characterizing the attributes of God. Where attributes are affected by the challenge of evil, metaphysical theodicy will characteristically turn to the ideal of wisdom to explain the reason why evil is allowed by an omniscient being. The benevolence of God has its rational limitations. Divine wisdom, for example, recognizes that too much of one kind of good, or too little of certain privations, or too great an interference on God's part prevents the maximization of good in the universe. The generative, restrictive, and vindicating functions of the cognitive ideal will be seen to operate in the logic of metaphysical theodicy, which we next examine.

What follows are some of the major themes which underlie both the classic and modern expressions of metaphysical theodicy. Our analysis is based on the writings of Augustine, Aquinas, and Leibniz, and in greater detail, on the relevant texts of their nonclassic contemporary counterparts, Henry Nelson Wieman, Charles Hartshorne, and Paul Tillich. We have confined our analyses to the philosophical aspects of theodicy in contrast to dogmatic theology and its special beliefs, such as the Fall. We are interested in showing how and in what sense the ideals of metaphysical theology employed in theodicy affect the biblical affirmations of God's goodness and His special relationship with man.

The Metaphysical Grand View

Goodness and/or Being

A major presupposition of classic metaphysical theodicy links goodness with being. They are denotatively the same. To be is good. Denial of one is denial of the other; not to be good is not to be. "For since being as such is good," Aquinas explains, "the absence of one implies the absence of the other.[16] Augustine's reading of the opening verses in Genesis, wherein each day's creation is called good by God, supports his claim that good includes every entity no matter how defective.[17] The biblical knowledge that the whole of creation and its parts are blessed with goodness is metaphysically translated into the virtual identification of being and goodness. *Omnium natura bonum est.* Ontological presence is intrinsically good.

Following the Neoplatonic teaching of Augustine, Aquinas asserts that goodness and being are the same, though goodness extends further than being in including both potential and actual things. Being may be spoken of as prior to goodness in the sense that it is conceived of earlier by the human intellect. Goodness, however, owns priority over being in that its desirability moves the agent toward some end. As a final cause, then, goodness may be spoken of as preceding being. Logically and functionally the two may be distinguished; ontologically they are the same.

But not all being or goodness is equal in value. Augustine's Neoplatonic vision organizes a hierarchy of being which is determined by the standards of form, order, and limit. The degree of goodness may be measured in accord with metaphysical criteria. In the scale of metaphysical value no absolute evil is registered. The metaphysical declension ranges from the absolute good to the not-so-good. However low the descent, its very existence testifies to its goodness, *malum est privatio boni.* This Augustinian-Thomistic view of *privatio boni* expresses the metaphysical optimism which celebrates the half-filled cup. Evil resides in the vacuum of being. It is "nothing," and God cannot be blamed for nothing at all. God only creates something and cannot properly be held responsible for the negativities which cling to it. Evil is not ontologically independent. Evil is parasitic, living off the good. So Aquinas, quoting Augustine (*Contra Julian* 1:9), argues that there is no possible source of evil except good.[18]

Goodness as a Whole

For metaphysical theodicy the importance of the identification of goodness with being and its scaling criteria of greater and lesser good is not confined to our arena in the universe. The superordinate referent of value is metaphysical. Goodness is exhibited throughout the hierarchy of the whole of being. No selected segment of being, therefore, can exemplify the fullness of God's benevolence. One must open one's perception wide to embrace the whole of being in all its variegated forms and degrees of existence. Such metaphysical comprehensiveness is necessary to overcome the provincialism of the partial view. Where goodness is represented by any one part of being alone, the image of divine benevolence is distorted. To be and to be good "are not the same absolutely" in any individual creature.[19] The whole, then, is better than any of its parts and better than the best of its parts. The metaphysical criterion of goodness includes a complexity of quantity and quality of being. The metaphysical view vastly expands the domain of its valuation; and with the enlargement of its scope comes a different principle of importance. The arena is not restricted to the fate of men and societies. The judgments of goodness are not made in terms of human standards or human satisfactions. Man, as a part of the whole of being, occupies a small area of God's creation. From a metaphysical *Gottanschauung*, the normal moral connotation of goodness appears culturally bound. Metaphysical wisdom promises to raise man from his parochialism, and therein lies one of the major consolations of its theodicy.

Things discretely examined are easily faulted. Seen within the larger context of the whole, their failings are wondrously transmuted into virtues, "and the whole itself, which is the universe of creatures, is all the better and more perfect if there be some things in it which can fail in goodness, and which do sometimes fail, without God preventing it."[20] To overcome the moral egoism of man, metaphysical wisdom favors the whole over its parts, the universal over the particular, the species over the individual. Consolation lies in widening man's view from his squinting view of finitude, the source of his despondence, to the sweeping vision of the All, the ground of his elevation.

The Logic of Inequality

The metaphysical mark of excellence is in the multiplicity and variety of things. The more the better; and the more varied, the more valuable. It is this appreciation of differentiation and plurality which at times provides metaphysical justification for the suffering of the weak. Logically, the ideal of ontological maximization requires an inequality of parts, including stronger and weaker, incorruptible and corruptible beings. God created all things unequal, and therein lies His goodness.[21] Were God to create the universe democratically, with equal status and power to all, the world would be doomed to static sameness. In his defense of God's plenitudinous creation, Aquinas maintained that "fire would not be generated if air was not corrupted, nor would the life of the lion be preserved unless the ass was killed."[22] His argument appeals to a view of good which claims to be wiser and wider than the provincialism which sees a world of lambs without lions and martyrs without villains. To extract tooth, fang, and claw from the universe is to eliminate the vital flaws and defects that stimulate and excite the fullness of creation. The spice of "evil" seasons the universe with a fullness of variety. If we alter our sights from the human subject to that of the graded whole, we may see "evil" in a new light. Such a change of view, the vision of the Divine Essence, is the task and happiness of man. Thus the tables are turned on those who would doubt God's existence because of the presence of evil. Without good, evil could not exist; without evil, goodness would be impoverished. Paradoxically, if there is evil, there is God. Leibniz echoes this logic in his declaration that to permit the evil, as God permits it, proves to be the greatest goodness.[23]

An aesthetic measure of metaphysical fecundity interprets the benevolent preferences of God. Accordingly Thomas knows that while an angel has more being than a stone, two angels are not therefore more to be preferred than an angel and a stone.[24] Or, as Leibniz speculated, "It is certain that God attaches more importance to man than to a lion, but I do not know that we can be sure that He prefers one man to the entire species of lions."[25] *La sagesse doit varier*.

Some Critical Observations

In a revealing passage in the *Summa theologica* we may see the use to which the perfection presupposition is put. Aquinas relies upon his particular idea of perfection to link actuality, or being, to goodness.

> The essence of goodness consists in this, that it is in some sense desirable. Hence the philosopher says: Goodness is what all desire. Now it is clear that a thing is desirable only insofar as it is perfect, for all desire their own perfection. But everything is perfect so far as it is actual. Therefore, it is clear that a thing is perfect so far as it is being; for being is the actuality of everything.[26]

To begin with, Aquinas's syllogism trades on the Janus-like character of the term "desirable." That all men desire goodness is, at best, a descriptive although questionable statement. When the alleged universality of men's desire slips into an assumption of its desirability, we have the marks of the "naturalistic fallacy." Descriptive and normative meanings are interchanged.

Note that it is the term "perfection" which serves to assimilate the evaluative sense of "desirable" and "goodness" into a descriptive meaning. The critical sentence, "But everything is perfect so far as it is actual," is stated as a self-evident proposition. It presupposes a particular Aristotelian idea of perfection. More important, where perfection and actuality are equated, as they are by explicit definition in Spinoza, reality serves as its own justification.[27] The normative sense of the good has de facto been supplanted by the Real. The perfection ideal has been used to identify desirable goodness with actuality. As a result, the normative moral connotation of goodness has been abandoned. The metaphysical ideal of perfection underlies the major arguments of metaphysical theodicy. In its identification with being and actuality, the metaphysical-perfection ideal has removed the moral grounds for criticizing the governance of the universe.

In broadening men's view of the universe, the metaphysical *Weltanschauung* tends to reduce the central importance of man. Metaphysical wisdom enjoins man to view himself modestly as *pars pro toto*. Plato's Athenian stranger offers a theodicy which calls upon men to recognize that they are "created for the sake of the whole and not the whole for their sake."[28] Armed with such wisdom neither Abraham nor Jeremiah nor Job would dare question the ways of God. And, indeed, in accordance with Maimonides' metaphysical approach, Job's agonizings are consequences of his false anthropological conceits. He wrongly supposes that man is the goal of creation, and judges his lot and God's goodness according to that presumption. Job's anguish is increased by his ignorance of God's intention "to give existence to all being whose existence is possible, because existence is undoubtedly good."[29] Where did Job look in judging the multiple evils of the world? He failed to look among the angels, the elements, and the celestial beings. He looked only at the limited sphere of mankind and projected its ills upon the whole of the universe.[30]

Our valuational stance is significantly altered by the metaphysical expansion of the range of our view. No segment of the universe is more privileged than another. To draw conclusions about the goodness of the infinite universe and its ruler from the limited domain of man is to fall victim to a moral anthropomorphism.[31] One of the major consequences of the cosmic view of creation is the loss of a discriminating axiological point of reference. Which disharmony cannot be readily justified by an appeal to ontological fecundity and complexity? Under what conceivable set of conditions, however tragic, will metaphysical theodicy admit that an event or act is evil, and not simply a contributory value to the enrichment of the universe? What of wasted, unrealized possibilities, cruel death, and unknown suffering? Freed from a human moral *locus standi* and the finite arena of earth, metaphysical theodicy can appeal, as Leibniz would have it, to "the infinite number of globes" where there may exist enough goodness to outweigh an entire earth of anguish. Leibniz is free to roam the infinite universe, "which must extend through all future eternity," in an easy quest for evidences of more and varied being.[32] The metaphysical perfection ideal is compatible with any state of affairs. The theodicy it proposes explains everything and anything in general. Particular and concrete sufferings are, in Hegelian fashion, swallowed up by the infinite and universal. As a theodicy its success is a triumph of invincible flexibility.

Theologians may welcome the metaphysical altruism which can justify the disorders of the part for the greater glory of the whole as an alternative to the parochialism of the humanistic point of view. They must be prepared, however, to surrender the high priority which biblical religion has assigned to moral good. Adoption of the metaphysical view and its presuppositions tends to deflate the value of the moral good. The ideal of metaphysical aesthetics is prepared to sacrifice the dull sameness of moral order for the excitement and stimulation of life. Against Pierre Bayle's vision of a God-ordered world unmixed with vice, Leibniz scorns the boredom which the superfluity of always singing arias from operas, eating nothing but partridges, drinking only fine wines brings.[33]

The supremacy of metaphysical good is articulated in its speculations concerning God's design. Thus Leibniz, in his theodicy, can argue:

> There is no reason to suppose that God, for the sake of some lessening of moral evil, would reverse the whole order of nature. Each perfection or imperfection in the creature has its value, but there is none that has an infinite value. Thus, the moral or physical good and evil of rational creatures does not infinitely exceed the good and evil which is simply metaphysical, namely that which lies in the perfection of the other creatures.[34]

The diminished status of moral good attends the displacement of man and human history as the vital center of God's concern. More than man's limited perception is transcended by the metaphysical view. The view which judges actuality by a moral, normative measure is equality transcended. The horizonless universe of metaphysics and its joy in ontological fecundity offers little room for tragedy, the serious base of Jobian protestation, or the need for redemption. Barth properly scores Leibniz for domesticating evil by easy conversion into instrumental value. The wolf has not only been made to dwell with the lamb, it has been transformed into a lamb itself.[35] Barth perceptively identifies the inadequacy of Leibniz's idea of perfection in its indiscriminate accommodation to all states of affairs. Speaking of Leibniz's metaphysical notion of perfection, Barth contends that "there is clear lack of a higher principle by which to select, decide and discriminate between the two [negative and positive aspects of creation] and therefore to say an unequivocal Yes which includes and expresses but also overcomes and transcends the unequivocal No."[36]

Barth's criticism of Leibniz may be extended to the logic which pervades metaphysical theodicy. Two seemingly contradictory notions of the ideal world appear within the corpus of metaphysical theodicy. On the one hand, the perfection of plenitude has so successfully rationalized finite evils that Aquinas is led to accept persecution and crime on the grounds that without them there would be "no patience of the righteous nor any place for a vindicating justice."[37] Without temptation and evil, men would not be free agents deserving of blame or praise. A perfect universe without physical or moral evil would be emptied of initiative, innovation, and spiritual growth.

Oddly, another Thomistic ideal of perfection, an eschatological vision, depicts a world of changeless bliss devoid of precisely those evils which were said to stimulate the joy of soul-making. Clearly a world where beasts of prey are all converted to herbivorous animals sated on straw and stubble is less plenitudinous than a world which includes the carnivorous. The Thomistic "state of immobility" which man cannot achieve in this life would seem hardly a proper reward for those who have been convinced that the struggling excitement of the cosmic plenum is truly ideal.[38] If sin and temptation are indeed logically necessary conditions in order to sustain man's freedom of choice, would not the eschatological promise of a life devoid of physical and moral evils deny men that very gift of freedom? If man's ultimate happiness beyond this life, as envisaged by Thomas, is like that of the angels, whose appetitive powers are moved entirely according to the order of reason, what logical obstacle could have prevented God from creating a free moral agent who cannot sin? Moreover, if this best of possible worlds justifies God's allowance of evil, which eschatological world could be better?

Do these dilemmas indicate some incoherence in Thomas's logic of perfection? We would rather suggest that the inconsistency is born of the amalgamation of contrary ideals of perfection, one stemming from a metaphysical view pressed by the need of a theodicy, the other from a biblical moral view called upon to justify undeserved suffering. It is this internalized duality of ideals which may urge Aquinas, in contrast to Leibniz, to maintain that given the things which actually exist, this universe cannot be better, though God could create another and better universe.[39] Leibniz's contrary position appears more consistent. From the single viewpoint of the metaphysical standards of excellence, the maximization and variety of beings serving as the measuring rod of goodness, God cannot create a better world.[40] But Aquinas retains, alongside the metaphysical ideal, a moral standard of excellence. According to the latter view, even if all evil cannot be eliminated because of metaphysical reasons, some suffering could be lessened.[41] The divine purpose moved by metaphysical goodness creates a universe wholly different from that which is motivated by the creation of moral goodness.

Chapter 4
Three Contemporary Versions of Metaphysical Theodicy

All discord, harmony not understood;
all partial evil, universal good;
and, spite of pride, in erring reason's spite,
one truth is clear, whatever is, is right.
--Alexander Pope

The perfection ideal of classical theism celebrates the self-sufficiency of God and favors those attributes which support that model of perfection. Other theologies find in growth and creativity the significant marks of excellence. For these the dynamic categories of process and evolution replace the more static categories of self-sufficent being. But as far as the problem of evil and the exculpation of God are concerned, the strategies of classic theism and "quasi-theism" remain essentially unchanged.[1] The theodicies of the nonclassical theologies still assess goodness by metaphysical criteria, except that goodness is tied to becoming rather than to being. What remains common to both is the suppression of the normal meaning of goodness through the conversion of its moral connotation.

Charles Hartshorne: Metaphysical Love and Metaphysical Beauty

Charles Hartshorne's process theology is particularly sensitive to both the biblical and the philosophical strands in historical theology. The perfection paradigm of classic theism favors permanence, simplicity, and actuality and is biased against change, plurality, and potentiality in God. The classic philosophic God of immutable self-sufficiency is judged by Hartshorne to be inconsistent with the biblical God, who allows Himself to be moved by prayers and the acts of His creation. The God of the Bible, unlike the God of the classic philosophers, enters into relational covenants with nations, and enjoys and suffers the lot of His children. According to Hartshorne, the theological failure to express a metaphysics reflective of the biblical view is due to traditional theism's reliance upon a one-sided, static metaphysics. He offers his own dipolar process philosophy as metaphysically supportive of the biblical God, who is "an all-loving, efficacious friend."[2] In his panentheism the attributes of being and becoming are harmonized so as to present one perfect being in whom two complementary qualities reside.

In what sense is Hartshorne's God a loving God? How does Hartshorne's God exhibit His efficacy and friendship? Whose friend is He, and does He take sides to protect the innocent tormented by evil? What moral significance, if any, is implied by Hartshorne's conception of divine perfection?

For Hartshorne, the controlling image of perfection is that of an inclusive process in which ideals are progressively realized and remembered. Hartshorne's panentheism conceives of God as an eternal-temporal consciousness, knowing and including the world. The mark of ultimate goodness is in the adequate taking into account of all possible and actual interests, each being given its due. "Maximal social inclusiveness" is the criterion of the goodness of the Supreme Being-Becoming. Evil is exclusion, the ignorance and ignoring of the interests of all things. God is aware of all, including all forms of evil. God "appreciates" the qualities of all things, "wishes all things well."

The plenitude principle of the *Timaeus* resonates in Hartshorne's process theodicy. For inasmuch as God's goodness is expressed in His concern for all, only a provincial anthropocentrism would have God declare His partisanship. "There may be those who think otherwise, who suppose that God can wish well to the sick child in such fashion as literally not to care about the woes of bacteria causing the sickness. But such persons, in my opinion, are thinking anthropomorphically about God, who must always relate Himself to absolutely all creatures."[3] This catholic compassion of God must be contrasted with the stolid impassibility of the Scholastic deity. Hartshorne's God grieves in all griefs.

The omnibenevolence of divine perfection governs God's providential wisdom. The God of process is not parochially bound. He balances, limits, and distributes powers with an eye toward maximal fecundity.[4] God's wisdom recognizes, on the one hand, that too much freedom increases discord, suffering, and pain; on the other hand, that concord gained by excessive external control would lead to a "loss of vitality, of depth of individuality, and of zest arising from creative capacities."[5] Ever open to growth and novelty, the Process-Perfection will not interfere with creation, but with persuasion holds a gentle rein, setting "wholesale limits to our eccentricities [and] guiding the world as a whole in a desirable direction."[6]

Observations and Critique

Masterful as is Hartshorne's intended translation of the biblical insight of God's nature into supportive philosophic categories, something vital to the biblical view is lost in the process. From the standpoint of the Bible, God's love is not nonpartisan. God takes sides with the victims of oppression, the slaves and orphans and widows of society. By contrast, Hartshorne's God expresses His love through His all-embracing appreciation of all things, lions and lambs, sick child and bacterium, villain and hero alike. God is our friend, but He is the advocate of our enemies as well. He cannot be said to intervene in history directly, not only because such controlling power would contradict the blessings of creaturely freedom, but because God participates in all beings and cannot be said to favor one form of being over another. Moreover, that which is evil for man may not be evil for God, whose master design transcends that of man's interest. "Human values emerge, sure enough," Hartshorne declares, "but are there not simian values, amoebic values -- and who dares to assign a first level of values?"[7] Such doubts would not likely be found in the biblical scale of values, wherein the human being is the sole creation formed "in the image of God" and set but "little lower than the angels."

From the impersonal vantage of metaphysics, God's "universal interest in interests" knows no such moral partisanship which would favor man over others. God's concern with maximizing zest, vitality, and creativity in the universe indicates another agenda than that presupposed in the liturgical and biblical outlook. It is not that God does not grieve for the killing of great numbers, in which He admittedly has a large share. "He merely has other values to consider also."[8] God's persuasive ways may well entail the sacrifice of human beings and their joys.

What God's values are cannot be articulated except in the most general terms. The criteria of good in terms of intensification of experience, variety, and growth are so vague and immeasurable that the slightest imagination can serve up a rationale for any state of affairs as metaphysically good. Ex post facto, what tragedy cannot be construed to possess a silver lining? And who but a mind reader capable of seeing the complex consequences of events into the infinite future could argue that a past catastrophe was so evil as to call into question the goodness of the process God? Given Hartshorne's process theology, Job's mouth would be quickly stopped up. In Hartshorne's own words, "are we to suppose that our [human] feeble love can tell us how infinite love must or might express itself, save in the vaguest and most general way?"[9]

Hartshorne's God is not a callous, aloof deity. God suffers the tragedies of His creations. But while awareness and compassion are necessary virtues, they are not sufficient conditions for determining the moral goodness of God. To know and to feel are not yet to act. Hartshorne's commitment to the metaphysical ideal of cognition leads him to substitute divine knowledge, memory, and aesthetic appreciation for the moral judgment and activity. Hartshorne places much stock in the redemptiveness of God's "cosmic memory," which preserves all values.[10] Nothing is lost because our sufferings are stored up in heaven and redeemed from perpetual perishing. Such retentive inclusion of values is a metaphysical virtue, but it is far removed from the faith in a salvific deity who inhibits evil and prospers the good.

God's Limiting Powers

Hartshorne's characterization of God's indiscriminate love of all things and maximization of freedom raises problems all too evident to the process theologian. While the catholic embrace of God's love includes bacteria and stricken children, he admits that he, and presumably God, would not deal with the conflict of interests evenhandedly. "On the other hand, should I have reason to kill an insect, I will not suppose that this has the same importance as killing a man."[11] While divine providence will not suppress freedom wherever it involves risk, it exercises limitations on excesses which threaten to cripple the promise of more life. "Divine providence may be a sort of superfate, but its function is to set limits to the free interplay of lesser individuals, which otherwise would be pure chaos."[12] But the exercise of providence's restraint upon the excess of evil is precisely the question which is hurled at theodicy. Hartshorne begs the question. Given genuine evil, are we then to assume that God deliberately did not set limits on human eccentricity in Auschwitz, Hiroshima, Biafra, Bangladesh? Or that these are not cause of gratuitous evil? Were no limitations set upon the ruthless men of the Holocaust because of God's metaphysical love, or are these ancillary events of the loftier project of God? Is divine nonintervention to be justified on the grounds that God has other values? If He will not or cannot use His coercive powers, does the metaphysical God care enough about humanity to exercise His powers of persuasion? If the persuasive powers fail so often and with many major events, in what sense is He significantly powerful, even if not omnipotent? Is His failure evidence of a malevolent persuasive power? And if so, are we not turned toward a radical dualism contrary to Hartshorne's monotheistic metaphysics?

Metaphysical Aesthetics: Whitehead

The metaphysical notion of divine love enables Hartshorne to justify the death of animals as providing them relief from boredom and to rationalize their swift death on the grounds that it is preferable to slow degeneration. Such strained justifications can perhaps best be understood by turning to Whitehead's metaphysical aesthetics, to which Hartshorne is indebted. For Whitehead "the real world is good when it is beautiful."[13] And perfection is maximum beauty, the harmonious inclusiveness of maximum intensity. His ideal is a footnote to Plato's principle of plenitude and a lever upon which his theodicy is raised. Storms and barbaric invasions, in themselves admittedly destructive, may be seen as contributory values to the adventures of ever new and increased perfection. The vision of the whole in process wipes out the terror of the part. Without conflict history would stagnate from the tedium of infinite repetition and degenerate through the stultifying tameness of life. "Beauty is a wider, and more fundamental, notion than truth. . . . The teleology of the Universe is directed to the production of Beauty. Thus any system of things which in any wide sense is beautiful is to that extent justified in its existence. . . . Thus Beauty is left as the one aim which by its very nature is self-justifying."[14] Some elements of discord are necessary to overcome what Whitehead calls "anaesthesia." The sufferings of discord may be seen as sacrifices to harmony. The intermingling of evil and beauty is metaphysically necessary and justified by an appeal to imperfection with aims higher than the lower levels of perfection. Progress, in God's eye, is based upon the experience of discordant feelings. Whitehead is clear that intensity of experience and variety are achieved "at the cost of eliciting vivid experiences of effective tones, good and bad. It makes possible the heights of Beauty and the heights of Evil; because it saves both from a tame elimination or a tame sending down."[15] It would be furthest from Whitehead's mind to consider that such a metaphysical theodicy could readily serve as a rationale for the repressiveness of totalitarian regimes. Yet Whitehead's abhorrence of boredom, tedium, and repetition and his adoration of adventure, excitement, and novelty lend themselves too easily to such use. Bemoaning the learning and learned taste of Hellenism, which replaced Greek genius by dull repetition, he can include "the irruptions of Barbarians" along with the rise of Christianity and Islam as vitalizing factors providing adventure in the search for new perfections.[16]

"It is in this way that the immediacy of sorrow and pain is transformed into an element of triumph. This is the notion of redemption through suffering, which haunts the world. It is the generalization of its very minor exemplification as the aesthetic value of discords in art."[17] The consequent nature of God salvages what appears to us as evil by transmuting its discordance into divine enjoyment. All of this strikes one as a manifestation of a divine aesthetic egoism. The individual who is a part of the larger pattern does not seem to count.

Whitehead's aesthetic theodicy informs us that what is evil for us is not evil for God. Against this is pitted the unconsoled and unconvinced protestation of other philosophers. "It is no help for present ills to know that God sees them in such a way that they are valuable for him. That my ill has an ideal counterpart in God does not help me very much as long as I am on earth and God is in heaven."[18] David Ray Griffin argues that such critiques by Stephen Ely, Peter Hare, and Edward Madden falsely accuse Whitehead's God of sacrificing human feelings for aesthetic ends. He maintains that Whitehead's aesthetic goodness needs to be understood "in a deeper sense" which entails harmony and includes moral goodness.[19] That deeper sense is at best ambiguous in Whitehead's writings, and read in the context of his theodical arguments points to a meaning beyond good and evil. To question the morality of beauty may be dismissed as a confusion of categories or as irreverence, but when the harmony of beauty is used to justify the sufferings of innocence, it remains the most pertinent of inquiries.

Hartshorne's dipolar metaphysics has, undoubtedly, provided a bridge between the biblical and philosophic understandings of the Supreme Being. His God is open to change, growth, and suffering and free from the absolute, passionless, and unchangeable character derived from the Greek idea of perfection. But the crucial element of the biblical ideal of perfection is not evident in his or Whitehead's process conceptualization of deity -- the moral character of God, who cares and acts to protect individuals and peoples from the onslaught of evil. Without the moral ideal of God and the expectations which it engenders, the very question which gave rise to theodicy is crushed. The problem of evil is not solved but dissolved by the transmutation of moral into metaphysical virtue.

Henry Nelson Wieman: The Theodicy of Metaphysical Naturalism

The perfection paradigm in Wieman's naturalistic theology centers on the creative sources of good. God is revealed, not beyond space and time, supernaturally, but through the process of creativity itself. Wieman's empiricism looks for God in the "creative event" which generates new qualitative meanings and which integrates and reorganizes them with the old ones and thereby transforms our lives into a richer and more inclusive whole. To the extent that an event has the character of intensity, complexity, and unity, it is good. But "creative good" must not be confounded with "created good." The instrumental and intrinsic kinds of "created good" are all culturally bound. They are limited in their connection and communication with other goods and in their capacity to generate new goods. Intrinsic "created good" is culture; instrumental "created good" is technological civilization. All "created good" is relative.[20] By contrast, "creative good" is absolute, transcending conditions of time, place, and position. The "creative good" of the process cannot be known beforehand.

To subject the creative process to our human judgment is an idolatrous exercise. Human efforts to control the creative process only result in evil. The creative process upon which we depend for our good proceeds without human consent or counsel. If we are wise and faithful, we will cooperate with it, though its consequences are unforeseeable.

Faith is required because the creative process often appears in opposition to human interests and standards of serviceability to man. It may be experienced as a hateful and fearful force running counter to all human desire.[21] But Wieman insists that the suprahuman, directive energy of the creative process must be allowed to transform us. Total and complete trust in its ways transforms our values and the very structure of events, so that "we come to love what we now hate, to serve what we now fight, to seek what now we shun."[22]

The creative event may not properly be judged because it judges us. However it may change our minds and hearts, it is to be trusted absolutely, for it "always produces good: it never fails."[23] What the absolute, creative elan may produce, man cannot by himself accomplish. The "qualitative meanings" unfolded through the creative process may be known, but only in retrospect. Looking back upon past events, we may see how the range of meanings has been expanded, how it has been integrated into the shared meaning of a wider community.[24] The growth of qualitative meaning is an objective, empirically observable phenomenon. If we can overcome the rigidity which binds us to particularistic norms and ideals, we will be opened to the ever-increasing "creative interchange" and intercommunication brought about through the creative process. Nevertheless, knowledge of divine creativity is as limited as any other empirically gained knowledge of events or processes. Consistent with his understanding of the unpredictable thrusts of creativity, Wieman cautions that our knowledge of God's total being is necessarily incomplete and subject to error.

Critical Observations

Wieman presents us with a specialized version of the principle of plenitude whose presuppositional character figured so centrally in classic metaphysical theodicy. Wieman has temporalized that principle. In place of the spatial whole comprising a variety of parts, he substitutes a temporal process through which flows a variety of events. Wieman's evolutionary system suggests a Plotinian emanationism in reverse; an upward thrust projected through history. The values of intensity, complexification, and increase of communicated meaning are worked out in an indefinitely prolonged sequence of generations and cultures.

Classic metaphysical theodicy focuses attention upon the infinite whole and thereby salvages meaning from the absurdity and tragedy of its parts. In Wieman's evolutionary theodicy, the eye is fixed upon the future, whose promise of growth rescues the apparent evils of the past. For classic theodicy, a prominent source of evil is traced to the narrowness of man's finite perspective; for Wieman, a major form of evil derives from man's fixation upon the "created good" of the past and present. The consolation of classic metaphysical theodicy calls for intellectual absorption of finite partiality into the comprehensiveness of the whole; for Wieman the way is through a commitment to openness, to a future which remembers past sufferings as necessary stages in a developmental hierarchy. It is to be expected that worshipful commitment to the source of good entails disappointments and sufferings. "We must be broken because there is a power which works in our lives to achieve a good we cannot compass and cannot discern, until some time later in retrospect it reveals the form of the new creation now invisibly emerging."[25] Wieman presents us with a familiar rationale, one we have seen in Hartshorne and Whitehead, for the allowance of suffering and conflict. Discord is necessary in order to generate deeper and more inclusive meanings. The principle of harmony is rejected by Wieman; it reduces the range and riches of man's appreciated good.[26]

The perfection presuppositions which inform Wieman's judgments concerning the character of the creative process are not far removed from the surface. He argues as if his preference for growth and risk over security and stability and for the values of society over those of the individual were empirically revealed in the directive of history. But we agree with the criticism of John B. Cobb, Jr., that Wieman's particular commitment to the good transcends his theory of value. Despite Wieman's criticism of those who would judge the creative process from the limited vantage point of human conventional ideals, his own commitment "depends upon a conditional historical situation for its acceptance."[27]

Wieman, it seems to us, finds himself in a double bind. He is caught up in an evolutionist *Zeitgeist* which places complete trust in process and creativity as the source of human good. At the same time, his perceptions are deeply informed by the values he has inherited from the Judeo-Christian ethic. It is the latter, we submit, which enable him to find such qualities as courage, kindness, generosity, and love within his abstract idea of "creative intercommunication."[28] Such altruistic qualities, which Wieman endorses, are not simply derived from empirical observation of process in history.

This tension between loyalty to the process of creativity and reverence for the traditional values of an inherited tradition appears evident throughout Wieman's writings. On the one hand, Wieman is persistent in declaring that man cannot set up his own criteria to judge the ways of the creative process. We are confronted with divine powers "qualitatively different" from human powers.[29] Creativity, we are reminded, is ontologically prior to both personality and mind. Its strivings are consequently not accessible to human imagination or purpose. Yet Wieman appears to know far more about the creative process and the measure and direction of its progress than is warranted by the ground rules of his own strictures. He knows that the direction of the creative process courses toward the increase of human "creative interchange."[30] He knows that widening the upper levels of the social hierarchy, increasing the diversity of intercommunicating persons and groups, apprehending and integrating communicated meaning into our lives are marks of progress.[31] Are these criteria extracted from an empirical observation of the flow of history, or are they smuggled in from prior religious and humanistic systems of value? Wieman's discriminating perception depends upon a selective principle based upon antecedent ideals of perfection. His values are not immaculately perceived through empirical observation.

By his own admission, the total cosmic process is not unified by a single direction of development.[32] Yet Wieman uses language which suggests that the creative process is somehow consistent in its purpose. Like Hartshorne, whose God "lures" and "persuades," Wieman speaks of a sovereign power which "guides," "condemns," "controls," "transforms," "produces," "makes demands."[33] His personifying language suggests an intending conscious agency organized for some unknown but supremely worthy end. It appears to us that Wieman's locution betrays his unresolved conflict. Though the demands are spoken of as if they come from some independent, responsible personality, they refer, strictly speaking, to events and processes of an unknowing and unknowable creative elan.

Wieman faces a more serious dilemma stemming from his metaphysical-religious allegiance to creativity and his attachment to Judeo-Christian morality. Following Wieman's criteria, we are not led to believe that the fruits of creativity need be moral in the usual religious sense of morality. May not complexity, greater freedom, and deeper appreciation of meaning be accomplished through the sacrifice of individuals or races or religions? Who can deny that infinite and unpredictable meanings can emerge out of terror and persecution? The values of appreciation, understanding, and communal cooperation are not incompatible with heartless and dangerous experiments with the lives of human victims. Wieman's "moral law" urges men to always act to provide conditions more favorable for creative interchange and expansion of meaning. It provides, however, no safeguards against those who, in the name of loyalty to transmoral destiny and global intercommunication, may justify genocide.

Wieman's moral law demands that "we live dangerously in the power and keeping of what destroys us as we are and re-creates us, often with suffering and transitory loss, into minds and communities that love beyond previous capacity to love and enter into every form of appreciation and constructive action."[34] Such courage and martyrdom may be justified where the morality of the one who demands, and of the end-in-view proposed, is known. But to plunge "into the jaws of destruction to be transformed into newness of life," without knowing the moral character of that newness, opens the door to madness.[35] Bereft of utilitarian, rational, or conventional moral criteria with which to judge the "demands" of the creative process, we are asked to submit our lives to incomprehensible cosmic energy. Why, particularly after our witness to the demonic destructive forces which brought on the Holocaust, should man forsake all for a good which "we cannot appreciate, trusting ourselves to the keeping of a power that works more creatively than the human mind"?[36]

In his discussion of the evolution of qualitative meaning, Wieman does little to alleviate our fears concerning the ambiguity of his judgments and their openness to malevolent exploitation. He admits that "only the few at the top can be the medium through which the creative event works most fully."[37] Acknowledging the unfairness to those at the bottom of the "hierarchy of sensitivity," he still judges the evil to be necessary in order to produce the richest fulfillment of value. What if the repression of some of those on the bottom can be shown to serve the creative process through further elevating the elite few? It is the other, traditional, morally conventional side of Wieman's philosophy which moves him to advocate that men fight this evil at "its source in the sub-human regions" whence it originated.[38] But how compatible is this call to resist the "sources external to human life" with the moral law which demands blind allegiance to the creative source? Would it not be a mark of arrant parochialism to resist the cunning of the process in history?

Wieman's theodicy for the creative process is simplified by his insistence that we know nothing about "final outcomes." All criticisms of the creative process may readily be dismissed as premature.[39] The consequences of events "cannot be foreseen and appreciated at the time the moral act is performed."[40] If so, we may ask, which point in time is the proper moment from which to judge the act in retrospect? Wieman has removed the temporal locus from which to evaluate the creative event. He has similarly removed the *locus standi* from which men can judge the event. For Wieman's goodness must remain absolute, immutable, and unqualified. It must be good from all sides of the perspective, from the point of view of man and that of the microbe. Such a catholic view de facto prevents the possibility of any criticism. No perspective in particular amounts to no perspective at all. Any critique of the alleged goodness of an event is too easily dismissed as stemming from a concern with a particular good or from a particular liking.[41] Where the well-being of no specified segment of creation may serve as a relevant test of goodness, justifications for evil abound. The metaphysical view, naturalist or supranaturalist, eschews any foreground. It is characteristic for it to draw all figures indiscriminately into the general landscape of the whole. Where the human figure is so absorbed into the background, the moral criterion of goodness is assimilated into the metaphysical overview. The careful reader of theodicies must continue to ask himself in what sense the term "good" is used, and, equally important, for whom it is good.

Paul Tillich: Theodicy and the Ground of Being

God alone is perfect. For Tillich this divine uniqueness is expressed in the equilibrium within being-itself wherein the dynamic and static elements of polarity are joined without possibility of disruption. Outside of God, a constant tension between individualization and participation, dynamics and form, freedom and destiny prevails, forever threatening disease through a one-sided domination. God alone is beyond the separation of essential and existential being.[42] The harmony of this perfection is not one of undifferentiated indifference achieved by blurring the distinctive values of the polarities or by emptying the positive attributes to reach the Absolute of Nothingness. Within God, symbolically understood, the full cordiality of the dialectics of life continues without the threat of conflict or separation which haunts the finite freedom of creation. The "id" of the abyss of the divine is united with the divine logos of the "superego" and made creative by the divine spirit.

By contrast, evil is disequilibrium. It is the imperfection measured by the Fall from ideal existence in which essence and existence are united. The metaphysical characterization of evil is separation (*Sonderung*). Phenomenologically it is experienced by man as an incessant civil war between the polarities. Aroused by freedom, man tears himself from his destiny; in his assertive dynamism he is separated from the structure of form; in his individuating will he is isolated from the stability of participation. Conversely, in choosing the passive elements of polarity, he represses the dynamic sources of his life. Guilt, skepticism, and the fear of death are modes of human anguish stemming from his estrangement from the ground of being and meaning.

The evil of separation is the tragic consequence of finite

freedom. The decision to exist as an individual, to actualize the potentialities only dreamt of in preexistent innocence, means to break the umbilical cord which ties him to the bliss of original unity. To awake from the state of pure potentiality and choose to realize his freedom, however, is an ambiguous act. For separation is at once the precondition for selfhood and the turning from the creator. Like the blessing of Balaam, the benediction of identity is quickly converted into the malediction of alienation. The free fall from essence to existence is paradoxically both descent and ascent. Alienation is drived from an inner necessity, not an external compulsion of finite freedom.

Tillich may be influenced by Schelling in this analysis of evil as "goodness in its division." Goodness and evil, for Schelling, are locked in interdependence. "The same thing which becomes evil through creative will (if it isolates itself completely to exist for itself) is in itself good, so long, that is, as it remains enwrapped in goodness and in the depths."[43] Schelling's metaphysical evil has its proper place as the primal basis of existence which strives toward actualization in created being. In Schelling's theogony, the unruly dark depths within God provide the essential conditions for the emergence of His personality. "All personality rests upon a dark foundation," which is relatively independent of God and controlled by Him.[44]

For Tillich, the evil of separation carries a similarly ambivalent value. It is a mixed curse, a universal condition in which actualized creation and estranged existence are two aspects of the same Fall. And for Tillich, a dialectical negativity within God, analogous to that of Schelling's, is exhibited in the presence of nonbeing within being, which enlivens the divine life in its process of overcoming nonbeing.[45]

One need not search far for the roots of a theodicy in a system which requires evil as a basis for the independence of good and in which evil exists unavoidably as the consequence of the creative act of freedom. Metaphysical evil cannot be condemned with the seriousness with which moral evil is denounced in the Bible. A theology which considers the sin of man to be virtually inevitable (John Hick), or too probable not to happen

(William Temple), or coincident with creation (Paul Tillich), tends toward some version of the medieval doctrine of *felix culpa*, the happy fault which leads to greater bliss.

Yet evil, for Tillich, is real. While he explains physical evils as simply the implication of creaturely finitude, and moral evil as the tragic consequence of creaturely freedom, he is aware of wasteful destruction which excludes some beings "from any kind of fulfillment."[46] Where is God in the midst of such absurdity? At this point, Tillich turns to the creative ground of being as "the ultimate answer to the question of theodicy."[47] The principle of divine participation in every life and in every moment provides a key to Tillich's theodicy. God as the absolute participant is not an interloper in man's life, bailing him out of crisis, nor is He a passive prescient spectator. His providential participation is more closely experienced in the "telos of creativity," in the inner creativity which is pulled toward fulfillment. God's providential character is in the ground of being which creates, sustains, and directs actualization of potentialities.

Critique

In what sense, then, is this ground of being moral? In what sense is this source of being and meaning a moral personality? To speak of a personal God means, for Tillich, "that God is ground of everything personal and that he carries within himself the ontological power of personality."[48] Consequently the answer to the question of God's morality or goodness calls upon God as the ground of everything good and of every moral act. God possesses the ontological power which is the source of goodness and morality.

Tillich's metaphoric terminology, e.g., "ground" or "source" or "origin," "root" or "basis," is ambiguous. Following one interpretation, these terms signify a neutral primal matrix. "Ground," for example, suggests an earth matrix out of which vegetation of all kinds may spring, wheat and weed alike. "Stolen seed sprouts as luxuriantly as seeds honestly acquired."[49] Every growth is "of" the soil, but the soil itself is "outside" its products and morally independent of them. Accordingly, "ground of being" refers to something underlying all things, in all things and yet beyond all things. Following another interpretation, however, terms such as "ground" and "source" designate an intentional force consciously aiming at deliberate ends. The "ground of being" and the "power of being," terms which Tillich uses interchangeably, imply a conscious activity which is subject to valuational judgment. Tillich himself is aware of the oddness of his terminology. He explains that "ground" is a limbo expression oscillating between cause and substance.[50] "Substance" comes too close to the kind of pantheistic immanence which robs man of freedom and God of His independence. "Cause" conveys too sharp a separation of God from His works. "Ground," then, ideally incorporates both the active and the passive elements of the polarities of being: free and destined, individual and participatory, dynamic and structured. But this both-and polarity is hard pressed by the problem of evil, where moral sensibility insists on a clarification of the providential role of divine participation.

How, for example, is divine participation expressed in the murder of a child? Tillich has credited Luther with transcending primitive personalism and approximating the meaning of ontological participation of the divine life in the negativities of existence. Luther saw God's participation in His giving power to the arm of the murderer to drive home the knife.[51] The ground of being, it would seem, participates indiscriminately in all things and events. Tillich's interpretation allows Luther to transcend far more than "primitive personalism." It seems to us that Luther here may have transcended the "moral" personalism of the biblical God as well. The ground of being as *anima mundi* is amoral, and its equal distribution of power to the wicked as to the just testifies to its universality, not to its morality.

At the same time, Tillich's providence "drives," "lures," "directs," or manifests the love and justice of the creative ground of being.[52] We have met these personalistic idioms before in the theologies of Hartshorne, Wieman, and Whitehead. How does such language square with the moral indifference of divine participation as exemplified in the arm of the destroyer?

It is at this point that Tillich's magnificent effort to correlate the biblical meaning of divine involvement with that of ontological participation falters. The biblical God may properly be understood as the ground of power and freedom, but fidelity to the biblical concept of divinity demands more of God. His ontological power needs to be implemented by moral decision and initiative on behalf of "the needy one who groans, the afflicted one who has no helper. He pities the poor and needy, the soul of the needy he delivers, redeems their souls from oppression and injustice; precious is their blood in his sight."[53] His discriminatory providential care must be removed from the unrighteous. It is insufficient to declare of the biblical glory of God's being that every act of courage is a genuine manifestation of the ground of being, "however questionable the content of the act may be."[54] It is not the metaphysical structure of being but the moral content of the act which is sustained by the biblical God of justice, and therein lies the trust in His goodness. Indeed, the Job-like victim inveighs precisely against the amoral participation of being in the courage of the barbarian.

Tillich's philosophical eisegesis of the Bible tempts him to ontologize biblical predicates of God out of their moral sense. In order to establish "the ultimate unity and profound interdependence" of biblical religion and ontology, he translates the personalism and concreteness of the Bible into the ultimacy and universality of ontology. "Personal logos," "love," "justice," "decision," "prayer" are converted into ontological concepts. Thus the biblical "nearness" of God to man is the merger of participation and individuation in His being.[55] But Tillich's divine "nearness" turns out to be closer to the Platonic participation of individual things in the universal essence than to the biblical meaning of God's "nearness" to those who call to Him in truth.

Nor does Tillich's analysis of God as the power of being who establishes the conditions for the emergence and maintenance of "personality" entitle him to endow God with personality. It is logically invalid to attribute personality to a being on the grounds of its power to generate personality. It is as illicit as would be the ascription of evil to God on the basis of evil's dependence upon the ground of being. To ascribe the character of personality to its causal source is erroneously to presume that the cause must resemble the effect. Equally, Tillich's contention that the universal logos present in all things and the personal logos of the Bible are "one and the same logos" can be maintained only by blurring the distinction between the metaphysical ubiquity of the former and the moral partisanship of the latter.[56]

For Tillich, as for Hartshorne, "love" is treated as an ontological concept characterized by inclusive unity and participation. It does not signify any special concern for mankind or for the oppressed. It is a love for each and every other "apart from higher or lower, pleasant or unpleasant qualities."[57] For him, divine "justice" is equally universal, functioning impersonally as an order of being. It neither commends nor condemns concretely but is evident in "the self-destructive nature of evil."[58] Tillich's claim that evil contains the seed of its own destruction is an ontological faith hardly adequate to morally justify the devastation wrought upon innocent others in the course of its self-destruction. But the critical point is that the ontological "love" of divine participation which is the same toward all, and the "justice" which is a universal order of being, are far cries from the "friend," "father," and "tutor" of man celebrated in religious consciousness. Feuerbach's criticism of the philosophers' idea of providence applies equally to Tillich's type of general benevolence and justice. That general providence which "extends itself equally to irrational and rational beings, which makes no distinction between man and the lilies of the field or the fowls of the air, is nothing else than the idea of Nature -- an idea which man may have without religion."[59] The true proof of providence according to religious faith is in the activity ordained exclusively for human salvation.

In examining Tillich's use of divine participation as an ontological concept, it is apparent that the relationship it describes in such traditional terms as "love" and "justice" is internal. "The creative ground of everything in every moment" cannot be said to have external relationship with its creatures, except in a poetic sense. The doctrine of participation in which all is in One and One is in all does not allow for creaturely independence. The creature is inseparably bound to the ground of being, however alienated it may become. As Tillich himself acknowledges, there is no place for the creature to withdraw or draw close.[60] For the ground of being is not an individual with whom one can enter into dialogic relationship, but is rather the ground of all possible relationships.

It follows from this ontological account that for Tillich the human-divine reciprocity running throughout religious literature is informed by a doctrine of internal relations. We are told, for example, that in true prayer "God is both he to whom we pray and he who prays through us."[61] The human-divine reciprocity is dissolved, so that in prayer it is God who "comprises both sides of the reciprocity."[62] If God is said to react to our prayers, it is only in the sense that He responds to His own powers which work through us. Here Tillich's doctrine of divine participation comes closest to a monism wherein the independence of the other is illusory. The ground of being is holy in the sense of unapproachability. Holiness for Tillich means that the moral and epistemic distance between Creator and creature is so great as to deny literal relationship with God. The holiness of God requires that in relation to God we "enter into a relation which, in the categorical sense of the world, is not a relation at all."[63] The biblical covenantal notion, which presupposes a more genuine independence of man and treats God "as a partner with whom one collaborates," Tillich regards as an insult to divine holiness.[64]

The theodicy in which the creative ground of being provides the ultimate answer requires acceptance of an ontological ground of being which itself transcends morality. Tillich's is another variant of metaphysical theodicy which de facto represses the claims of moral consciousness.

By Way of Summary: Abraham Maslow and Peak Cognition

There is more than philosophical attractiveness in the metaphysical approach to theodicy. There are psychological gains in seeing the universe through God's eyes, *sub specie aeternitatis.* For one thing, the private sufferings of the lone individual are through the metaphysical perspective raised to cosmic significance. The personal loss is invested with metaphysical dignity by assuming its place in the larger scheme of things. Paradoxically, along with this new elevation of individual anguish as a contributory event in the enfoldment of God's cosmic design there is a reduction of egocentric concern. There is consolation in a metaphysics which simultaneously dismisses the parochial character of my pain and raises it to significance as a contributory part of God's plan.

In reading Abraham Maslow's phenomenological account of "peak-experiences" we were struck by the affinity between the psychology of such experiences and the philosophy of metaphysical theodicy. Both see the world beyond the usual judgments of good and evil. Both find comfort in a transcending meditation of the self in the world. In his *Toward a Psychology of Being,* Maslow discusses a list of traits which characterize the perceptions of people having peak-experiences. In the cognition of being (B-cognition) of peak experiences, the object experience tends to be seen "as a whole," as a complete unit, "detached from relations, from possible usefulness, from expedience and from purpose."[65] The entire universe is experienced as if it were "independent not only of them but also of human beings in general."[66] The perceptions are thus relatively detached or ego-transcending. The reduction of the importance of human being in such experiences is similar to that experienced by the theological metaphysician. The centering point in the psychological account, as in the metaphysical formulation, is outside the human self and fixed to an independent reality.

Unlike normal perception, B-cognition is nonevaluating. Normal figure-ground relationships no longer hold because the percept becomes "for the moment the whole of Being." We have observed that the metaphysician similarly views the world as a landscape without a foreground, and that this enables him to see the universe nonjudgmentally. Things are what they are. Maslow's subjects "accept reality" as being-in-itself, in its own right. Reality is neither "for" nor "against" man. Accepted impersonally for what it is, Maslow's subjects explain, reality presents no ethical problems. "It is in principle possible to admire the beauty of the flood or the tiger in the moment before it kills or even to be amused by it."[67] We have earlier observed how metaphysical aesthetics is able to look at evil as the contrasting shadow of light which adds color to the plenitudinous universe.

The B-values of peak-experience cognition include wholeness, completion, beauty, and self-sufficiency. The whole of being is good or neutral, while evil is seen as a partial phenomenon. In this insight of wholeness, there is felt a "fusion and unity of the old trinity of the true, the good, the beautiful."[68] "Is" and "ought" are collapsed, and old dichotomies, polarities, and conflicts are transcended. Maslow could as easily have been writing of the metaphysical vision when he describes the resolution of splits which is experienced by his subjects. "The more we understand the Whole of Being," he explains, "the more we can tolerate the simultaneous existence and perception of inconsistencies, of oppositions and of flat contradictions."[69] When the spectacles of the near-sighted are removed, all the blemishes of evil fade away.

Maslow observed that B-cognition is characteristically "more passive and receptive than active." We have commented on the metaphysical orientation to life, which calls for no activist transformation of the world and does not conceive of God in such terms. It acquiesces in the status quo with the benign wisdom of "choiceless awareness."

Seeing is better than blindness. However painful the cognitive experience may be, it is preferred to the normal perception of things. Maslow's subjects regard the experience as self-validating, requiring no justification beyond itself. The metaphysical drive to know is analogously content in cognition which is regarded as an end in itself. Maslow, of course, is offering no theodicy and advocating no view on life's meaning. He is describing phenomenologically a type of experience and cognition. But the metaphysical perfection ideal of God and the experience of wholeness and perfection of Maslow's self-actualizing persons are kindred spirits. They share the holistic vision which flattens out the abrasive edges of life.

Chapter 5
Theodicies of a Personal God

How are we to avoid both an easy pessimism on the one side and a no less easy optimism on the other? How are we to think God's lordship even over nothingness with the necessary confidence and yet also the required humility. Nor is the truth to be sought in a central position of neutrality between these claims; for all are of equal urgency. Nor can we overcome the contrast between God's holiness and His omnipotence by meditation.

--Karl Barth

Paralleling the cognitive drive to know is the drive to be known. The latter is objectified in the image of an ideal divine personality in relationship with the human personality. What is sought is the felt recognition of self by the divinely significant Other. Whether the believer is enlightened or remains ignorant of the nature of that Other is secondary to the awareness that he is not ignored. Rewarded or punished, he knows himself to be understood, to be remembered, to be singled out. However stringent the chastisement and punishment, he knows himself to be in the foreground of the cosmic landscape. Whether lowered by the fall or raised by redemption, he enjoys divine attention. The recognition thirsted for is not stated by the metaphysical model of self-sufficient omniscience or the impersonal relationship of part to whole, or of the relative to the absolute. Neither substance nor idea, only personality, can affect the communion with the human personality which would satisfy the need to be known. The supereminent personality believed in is a far cry from Thomas's God in whom "there is no relation to creatures, but a relation only in idea."[1] The living God of the testaments expresses perfection in being personally involved with His creatures, suffering their anguish and intervening in their history. The significant Other feels, wills, commands, judges, forgives, rewards, punishes, hears, and responds; in short, such a divine knower is a personality.[2]

The ideal of wisdom, immutability, and causal power as assigned to the supreme metaphysical being takes on another meaning when ascribed to the divine personality. The wisdom of the personal God is not introspective, but is expressed in His "probing the secrets of the heart."[3] The immutability of the divine person is not founded in His metaphysical simplicity, but in the constancy and trustworthiness of His word. His causal efficacy is not that of an unmoved mover passively drawing beings toward their realization like iron filings attracted to a magnet. The divine personality performs miracles, exercises will, elects and rejects nations and men.

The object of devotion elicits different responses according to the dominant need of the believer. Toward a metaphysical God, the proper posture of prayer is contemplation and meditation. Toward a personal God, prayer is communion and response. Personality enables accessibility. A personal God is available to be petitioned. He moves and in turn may be moved by persons. A personal God need not be cognitively expressed. He may be liturgically addressed. One can address a person, pray to a person, and hope for a response from a person.

Personality and Covenant Relationship

What presuppositions lie behind addressing God as a Thou? Henry Aiken contends that to speak of deity as personality means that "we automatically treat it as an agent to whom certain obligations are due and from which the fulfillment of corresponding obligations may be expected."[4] To know that we deal with a personality means that He will not act capriciously. Reasonable expectations relative to His behavior seem to follow from the ascription of personality to the Supreme Being. We are not as convinced as Aiken that personality always entails the obligatory relationships which he suggests. It may be argued that personality endows the agent with cognitive, conative, and volitional powers without making any claims as to its moral character. But if we derive the meaning of addressing God as person from the bulk of Judaically interpreted liturgical and scriptural literature, a stronger case in favor of Aiken's position may be made. In one such major reading of testament and liturgy, the Thou addressed is understood to be a morally responsible personality, eminently trustworthy. The covenant relationship into which He enters with man is morally intelligible, its conditions binding upon divine and human personalities. In the context of the covenant, the essential predicate of His personality is morality, not omnipotence of will. The greatness of God's personality is revealed in the self-limitation of His absolute power so that He may enter into a proper moral relationship with man. The personal God of the Bible is bound neither to *moira* nor to *ananke*. He voluntarily submits Himself to the ethics of righteousness. The original meaning of *brith*, or "covenant," T. Begrich explains, refers to an arrangement of partners unequal in status but one in which the more powerful "binds himself to a certain attitude towards the less powerful on condition that the less powerful fulfills his part of the agreement."[5]

God's personality is not used to derogate man's moral sense or to demonstrate His own amoral freedom. God wishes man to understand Him morally so that he can emulate Him morally. God informs Abraham of His plans for Sodom and Gomorrah, "for I have known him to the end that he may command his children and his household after him, and they may keep the way of the Lord, to do righteousness and justice."[6] Nothing vitiates the moral purpose of the covenant as much as the envelopment of God in a mist of supramoral inscrutability. It is the measure of the greatness of His personality that He is morally intelligible. "For the Lord will do nothing, but He revealeth His counsel unto His servants the prophets."[7] For Jeremiah, God wishes to be known. To know God is no metaphysical exercise. It means to imitate God's moral concern for the weaker vessels of society. "Did not thy father eat and drink, and do justice and righteousness? Then it was well with him. He judged the cause of the poor and needy; then it was well. *Is not this to know Me? saith the Lord.*[8]

The lingua franca between the two personalities of the covenant, God and man, is morality. Man understands and shares a common vocabulary with God. The universe of discourse is not metaphysics but morality. Metaphysically God may remain a mystery; morally no such epistemic distance is allowed. God's punishment of Sodom and Gomorrah must make moral sense. Equally moral is Abraham's contention: "That be far from Thee to do after this manner, to slay the righteous with the wicked, so that the righteous fare as the wicked. Far be that from Thee. Shall not the judge of all the earth do right?"[9] The biblical presuppositions which legitimate this human-divine encounter include:

a. The moral nature of the divine personality
b. The moral competence of man
c. The moral comprehensibility of the covenant

These presuppositions authenticate the confrontation, which otherwise would be dismissed as an act of insolence. Where the divine personality is taken to embrace a moral meaning, the dissent is justified by God's recognition of man's moral capacity to know right from wrong. The covenant then is dependent upon the juridic principle of "free negotiation, mutual assumption of duties and full recognition of the equal rights of both parties concerned with the covenant."[10] The moral personality of God confers dignity upon man and assures the inalienable rights of the covenant's co-signatories. The patriarch's critique, far from being an act of insubordination, is rooted in his commitment to God as the exemplary moral personality. He judges God by God. So the psalmist will admit to no guilt on the part of the people slaughtered as sheep in confronting God.

> We have not forgotten Thee, or been false to Thy covenant. Our heart has not turned back, nor have our steps departed from Thy way that Thou shouldst have broken us in the place

> of jackals and covered us with deep darkness. If we have forgotten the name of our God, or spread our hands to a strange God, would not God discover this? For He knows the secrets of the heart. Nay, for Thy sake we are slain all the day long and are accounted as sheep for the slaughter. Rouse Thyself! Why sleepest Thou, O Lord?[11]

A talmudic discussion (*Sotah* 48) reports that the Levites of the First Temple recited this very psalm to awaken the slumbering God.

The Bible and the rabbinic tradition do not dismiss such bold positions as acts of hubris or *lèse majesté*. If Job is resolved not to falsify his moral claims of innocence so as to justify God; if he continues to declare, "I hold my righteousness and will not let go"; if God repudiates his friends, it is on the grounds of the moral covenant of reciprocity which informs their relationship. The bilateral covenant signifies that there is no double standard, one for God and one for man. As far as moral behavior is concerned, it means that one standard of righteousness extends vertically between man and God as it does horizontally between man and man. The covenant is one in heaven as it is on earth. Consequently, in the Bible, the moral predicates ascribed to God's personality do not appear to be qualitatively different from those assigned to man's. Goodness is univocally applied. Certainly God's goodness is not man's in a quantitative sense. Divine justice is more reliable, more trustworthy, more efficacious than man's. But the difference appears as a matter of degree, not of kind. Indeed, the qualitative sameness of the moral attributes enables man's moral *imitatio dei*.

The dialogue which issues out of the covenant relationship is intensely personal. Questions of blame and responsibility for evil abound under the conditions of such interpersonal intimacy. Anthropomorphisms, some biblical theologians contend, are more precise than analytic theologic categories because the God of Scriptures cares about man. The purpose of anthropomorphism, Ludwig Kohler informs us, is

> to make God accessible to man. It holds open the door for encounter and controversy between God's will and man's will. It represents God as person. It avoids the error of presenting God as a careless and soulless abstract idea or a fixed principle standing over against man like a strong silent battlement. God is personal. He has a will. He exists in controversy ready to communicate Himself.[12]

The believer in such a personal God knows that even in the midst of his suffering he has to do with no general principle, but with the personal word of God. He has to do with no academic conception of a being fettered by logical principles or constrained by fate. His God not only knows but cares; not only appreciates but acts.

The thunder and lightning of the Holocaust have revealed the disfigurations of that living relationship. How is the I-Thou relationship to be sustained after the onslaught of evil and the silence of God? What may be said of the living God so as to defend His constancy, His keeping the word of His covenant? What interpretations will the biblically grounded theodicies offer the moral predicates of the perfect personality?

Karl Barth: Yahweh, Elohim, and the Book of Job

In the wake of metaphysical theodicy, the lone figure of modern Job remains unconvinced. Metaphysical evil, the aesthetics of plenitude, the notion of privation ignore his broken covenantal dream. Metaphysical theodicy knows nothing of his living God whose arena is history and whose major characters are personalities, corporate and individual. Not in metaphysical speculation but in tracing the footsteps of God in history is the revelation of God's ways to be found. "And I will take away My hand, and thou shalt see My back: but My face shall not be seen."[13] Not via the impersonalism of metaphysics but through the loving examination of God's involvement in history is "His-story" revealed (Buber). Whatever theodicy is to be established must be grounded in the events of history, wherein is inscribed the moral theology of the Divine Author.

The religious domain is history as interpreted by the wisdom of the Word. Suffering may be variously interpreted as retributive, rewarding, probational, or disciplinary -- but it is never accidental, unjust, or incidental to man. The ultimate judgment of historical events is traceable to the benevolent wisdom of the personal sovereign of the universe. The Lord of History is a personal God who forms light, creates darkness, and makes both peace and evil.[14] Assyria is the rod of His anger as surely as Cyrus is His anointed staff. Secular interpretations of historical events may content themselves with superficial explanations; the religious interpretation is based on no external necessity but rather upon a moral teleology. Nebuzaradan, the conquering Babylonian general who vanquished Jerusalem, may boast of the superiority of his forces, but the Bible knows that the fall is morally caused. Consonant with this moral teleological perception of events, the rabbinic tradition informs the arrogant general that he has slain a dead people, burned a Temple already consumed, ground flour long ago ground.[15] Genesis and destruction, victory and defeat, exodus and exile, election and rejection, life and death are all traceable to God's verdicts upon man, individually and collectively, in the courts of history. "Doth evil befall a city unless the Lord hath done it?"[16]

Not metaphysics but history, not the universe in general but man in particular, is the focus of the Bible and the orientation of personalistic theodicy. While God is the creator of all creation, His significant other is man. No metaphysical referent will distract the biblically grounded theologian from the central dialogue between the personal God and man, between Yahweh-Elohim and Job.

Karl Barth's theological exegesis of the Book of Job demonstrates the extraordinary role which the idea of divine personality plays in his theodicy.[17] For Barth, the moral of the Book of Job is the discovery that in dealing with God we have to do with a totally unique personality, with a subject who alone offers content to the predicates ascribed to Him.

To follow Barth, at the outset of the Jobian drama Job knows only Elohim, the *Deus revelatus*, God as partner and friend. His idea of God has been formed and confirmed by benevolent experiences in life. Now he suffers terrifying afflictions. He is bewildered, because as a believer in one God he knows that whatever sorrow befalls him comes from God. As a monotheist he knows that suffering comes from no secondary god. Job's faith and honesty force upon him the recognition of a relentless, cruel, hostile force. At the same time, the memory of Elohim and the covenantal compact supports his protestation against this alienating power. He appeals to the co-signatory of that "record on high" for witness and vindication.[18] Only at the conclusion of the dialogues with man and the voice out of the whirlwind does Job come to know the identity of this alien and unpredictable form. Yahweh, the concealed personality of the divine, is the same as Elohim. In Job's moment of truth, the "two gods" are known as one. Adversary and advocate inhere within the same personality. Through this shock of recognition Job finds his reconciliation with God. He has come to believe in Elohim despite his belief in Yahweh, and in Yahweh despite his belief in Elohim.

To become aware of the oneness of Yahweh-Elohim is to overcome the inner conflict which tears apart Job's fidelity. "Far from the Word uttered by Yahweh provoking or even fostering division in Job's thought of God, it restores and re-establishes the Unity which is so severely threatened."[19] This inner unity has been achieved through Job's heroic surrender to Yahweh as "the ruling Subject in the history of Job."[20] Such willing and unconditional subordination to the divine subject is the triumph of faith. In obedience to the self-revelations of Yahweh, in the acceptance of His ways without attempting to judge them, Job finds his true freedom. He is free from the futile efforts to understand, justify, or contend with the ultimately inscrutable manifestations of the distinctive personality.

For Karl Barth, the need for theodicy is itself a symptom of man's enslavement to moral and logical criteria and norms irrelevant to the conduct of the divinely unique One. Yahweh neither requires nor asks for Job's "understanding, agreement or applause."[21] The very question which underlies the alleged need for theodicy is presumptuous. The "message of the cosmos" whispering through the whirlwind informs Job that he is not the center of the universe, that he has nothing to do with its direction, that he is incompetent and irreverent in thinking he can judge its teleology.

What then of the old covenant which promised men security and moral intelligibility of the world? That solidity Barth judges to be "static." Its monodimensional character is superseded by a dynamic, changing relationship.[22] True relationship is alive with unpredictability. The divine other is subject personality, not impersonal moral or metaphysical ideals. The divine person cannot be made perceptible to man, reasonable and amenable to human standards, without reducing His dignity. The true Subject of faith is Yahweh, the unique personality who will not be confined to any limits outside Himself. Man's expectation level must accordingly be opened beyond the limitations of his objectified ideals. With Yahweh, one must be prepared to live in surprise. For man knows nothing of the immanent autonomy of God's purpose.

In the beginning Job had only half a god, and his fidelity to such a partial deity led to his alienation. Loyalty to Elohim is idolatrous and ultimately self-idolatrous. And Barth, while understanding Job's honorable defiance against Yahweh, will not justify it. "Ungodliness does not cease to be such because it is ungodliness in what is good."[23] Nor is Barth easier on Job's comforters. Their apologetic is filled with sacred cliches dependent upon their acquaintance with Elohim alone. For all their obduracy in clinging to the good and just even in the fire of affliction, they have straitjacketed the divine personality. They have frozen the fluidity of God's will and acts into abstract, general, universal attributes -- all "unhistorical terms."[24] In moralizing God's ways they have programmed Him into a safe and predictable moral machine. God's repudiation of their apologia Barth takes as a warning against institutional truth. In binding the unconditional freedom of the divine subject to the moral predicates they have made sport of His sovereignty.

It would appear that the logic of Barth's harmonization of the two gods results in a subordination of Elohim to Yahweh. One cannot come to Yahweh through Elohim because the latter refers to the generic name of His righteousness, wisdom, and goodness. Through the generality of Elohim-attributes we remain with dead, changeless essences, knowing nothing of His initiating revelations in the dynamics of historic events. Elohim-centered, we know nothing of the Lord who stands over against us, conformable to no antecedent behavior, the absolute source and norm of all the good. For the friends of Job, "He is not Yahweh and as such Elohim-Shaddai, as such righteous, wise and powerful in what is always a definite and limited sphere, as such operative and manifest in these His attributes."[25] For Job's friends, the predicates decide the subject. Therein lies concealed the deepest heresy of religion, according to Karl Barth.

Personality as Subject

Barth's account of the Job story and the relationship between Elohim and Yahweh exemplifies his major concern for the proper relationship of predicates and subject in theological propositions. It will preoccupy our discussion of predicate theology in our final chapter. Yahweh is the paradigm of the divine subject which spawns a collection of divine predicates. For Barth, it is critical that the subject-predicate relationship remain irreversible. The subject and only the subject determines the predicates. Without the subject, the predicates are lifeless and their meaning undetermined. Barth is ever concerned lest the predicates of divinity, once assigned meaning independent of the subject, become the measuring rod of God. Once they are given separate status, characterized unequivocally, the subject is open to judgment according to the sense of the predicates. For Barth opposition to the biblical God, whose being, acts, and love forever are "His own," may be traced to the false autonomy claimed by the predicates of divinity. Naturalism, idealism, romanticism, humanism err in common by allowing the priority and primacy of the predicates of divinity over that of the divine subject. In opposition to such subordination of the subject, Barth announces that

"Strictly speaking there is no divine predicate, no idea of God which can have as its special content what God is. There is strictly speaking *only* the Divine Subject as such and in Him the fitness of His divine predicates."[26] The truth and meaning of all predicates remain the prerogative of God as the one subject. Only the subject gives meaning to the what.

The subject is the "Who," best characterized as personality. But "personality," we are cautioned, is an attribute borrowed from our experiences with human persons. The meaning of personality as applied to the Divine Subject cannot be gained by analogy from below upwards, but is acquired derivatively from His self-disclosure. Only God is Subject, only God is personality. "Not we but God is I."[27] We can therefore learn nothing from the claim that God is or has personality if we think we understand what personality means in itself.[28] God as personality prevents man's predicate worship. Despite its pious sounds, fidelity to universal and comprehensible predicates is but a circuitous adoration of our objectified projected values.

In examining the attempts of those philosophers and theologians who would deny attribution of personality to God, Barth detects a secret rebellion against the autonomy of the predicating subject. Behind the efforts of Hegelian theologians to defend the absoluteness of the Infinite Spirit from the compromising personality, he sees a subtle preemption of God's exclusive controlling function by the human personality. For them, human personality, despite its finitude, becomes the true I who wills and knows and names the acts of God. The Divine Subject is domesticated by the predicates known by man and used to determine the shape of God. Even those who ascribe personality to God but simply as an appended predicate torn from man's noblest part (H. Siebeck, R. Rothe, Lotze, and Ritschl) rob God of His exclusive autonomy. The origin and selection of the predicate is still man's. In genuine faith, as Barth conceives it, the predicates of God are revealed in concrete, particular relations; but all the predicates are entailed in the subject and are not refutable by any conceivable experience. In this sense, Barth's subject theology appears analytic; that is, the predicates are entailed in the subject. The subject is unconditionally true and beyond definition. To properly ascribe personality to God is to recognize something which precedes all human predications.

The limitations of Job and his comforters are revealed in their appeal to the predicates of an accessible Elohim. Yahweh is, however, a veritable predicateless subject. Job would not have complained nor would his friends have offered defense of God had they not relied on the independent meaning of His predicates. Only the subject may judge. Man, as the object of that judgment, can properly only receive and accept. The ground of the critique of God is removed at its foundation.

We are presented with a hard disjunction: theology judges either the subject according to the predicates or the predicates according to the self-disclosure of the subject. For Barth the choice is unambiguous. The subject is the unquestionable norm and criterion of the goodness of its imperatives.

What then of God's self-disclosure? Have we no knowledge of God's attributes after the revelatory self-manifestation of the subject? Is there no constancy in God's justice or mercy? Barth cannot endow even the revealed predicates with immutability lest they thereby serve as measures of God's future conduct. No external rules of logic or semantic order or moral standard can judge His self-endured constancy. However God's actions may appear to contradict His earlier self-revelation, they are internally consistent in Him. "The fact that He is one and the same," Barth contends, "does not mean that he is bound to be and say and do only one and the same thing."[29] Who then possesses the true measure of sameness to judge the constancy of an absolutely free, living personality whose decisions are flexible? No epistemic guarantees are offered to man by faith in the unique and dynamic personality. Metaphysical and moral predicates hold no fettered meaning over His actions. Accepting the mobility of His actions, the man of faith must surrender all claims to knowledge of the character of His immutability. Anticipation of His future acts based upon past performances presupposes a uniformity of divine nature less justifiable than the scientist's dependence upon the uniformity of nature. Man must be prepared to encounter His will ad hoc. He cannot make any deductions from the singularity of His concrete self-revelations, neither as to His essential character nor as to His future conduct. It may well not happen the same way a second time; indeed, the second time may contradict what man has taken to be the meaning of the original self-manifestation. With no constant predicates ascribable to the subject, man's false security is shattered. For they provided a stability surreptitiously based upon the human conceit in his cognitive grasp of the elusive subject. However, if the man of faith trusts in the perfections of God, he can never be completely free from the suspicion that the divine personality has chosen to reveal himself "in this or that form" in a "kind of sport," without disclosing Himself in reality, without giving us any pledge that in Himself He is not perhaps quite other than He appears.[30]

What does it amount to, then, that God has revealed Himself to be "right, friendly and wholesome"? How does faith in God's goodness or His love affect man's expectations? Again, we return to Barth's insistence that the theological propositions of faith are not to be inverted. "God is love" does not mean that "love is God." Love itself is undefinable. "God is love" means that our attention is to be directed toward the one who loves. The Who, not the what, must be our ultimate concern.

We know nothing about God's love. Consequently, we have no right to inform God that killing, rejecting, and condemning man "from the very beginning, from all eternity" is contrary to the idea of love.[31] If anything, we must learn from God's unconditional love how we are to love the subject without any regard to the predicates. For God's true love is not tied to the worthiness of the object loved. The "sovereign love" of the subject is not dependent upon the lovability of the predicates of the other.

Helmut Gollwitzer elaborates upon this Barthian motif by distinguishing between erotic and genuine love. Erotic love is the love of the object's predicates, for it is directed towards the other only as "a bearer of the worth."[32] The other must be worthy of our love. Genuine love is interested in the other as subject, irrespective of the predicates. Such unconditioned love is focused upon the "ego" of the other without regard to its qualities. The subject or personality of God cannot be translated into predicates.

Barth intends to preserve the freedom and uniqueness of God's sovereign "I" by negating the independent ontological and axiological value of the attributes. Otherwise, God is simply summed up as a collection of ultimate values and potencies. Such values apprehended, approved, and worshipped by man mask the conceit of self-love and self-sufficient knowledge. There are no sources outside God's self-revelation that can help us understand the divine perfection.[33] The analogical nature of language must not be taken so seriously that it is confounded with the inner nature of God.

In addition to his biblical exegesis of the problem of evil, Barth surprisingly introduces a speculative account of evil. We share John Hick's judgment that Barth's conception of evil as *das Nichtige*, "uncreated Nothingness," is more a mythic notion, one which violates his own strictures against such theorizing.[34] Nevertheless, Barth's biblical and speculative treatments of evil both share his consistent emphasis upon the utter incomprehensibility of evil. The sinister, resisting element as portrayed by Barth in his concept of *das Nichtige* eludes human knowledge and control. Nothingness cannot be handled by man conceptually or existentially. Only the divine subject can comprehend and overcome the alien adversary. Evil is supramoral. It stands above the moral categories of human understanding. It is inexplicable and inaccessible to the human creature.[35]

The self-reliant *ego cogito* only stands in the way of describing the real adversary with whom he thinks he can cope. Barth's complaint against the moral philosophers from Leibniz to Sartre is that they seek to manage evil by rationalizing it. They have thought variously to adapt to evil, to remove the terror of its sting, to view it as an esoteric instrumental good, to accept its inevitability, to resolve to live with it as something offering peace and security. Barth's biblical and mythic interpretations are consistent in their affirmation that the understanding, conquest, and removal of nothingness is primarily and properly God's own affair.

Barth's Use of Divine Personality

The Barthian solution to the problem of evil amounts to the dissolution of the problematic itself. The presuppositions of the Jobian expostulation with the divine are attacked as presumptuous. As we have seen, Barth's conception of the divine personality assumes the primacy of the subject and an irreversible relationship between it and its predicates. His exegesis of the Book of Job is faithful to the absolute dominance of the divine personality. That which Barth describes as Job's final acknowledgment of the identity of the two Gods is in fact achieved by the absorption of Elohim by Yahweh, by the assimilation of the predicate by the determining subject. Barth's analysis suggests the need for an anthropodicy, not a theodicy, for a justification of man's sinfulness, not of God's justice. The proper relationship of nature to the radically transcendentalized, totally other subject is, in Peter Berger's sense of the word, "masochistic."[36]

For all its contrast with the alleged impersonalism of metaphysical God-ideas, the living personality of the Barthian God is no more compassionate toward man or more supportive of the ideals of human personality. The common claim that the understanding of God as personality transfers to man greater dignity than does the metaphysical God-idea is not borne out in Barth's personalism. After Barth, we are not convinced by Herbert Richardson's claim that "the integrity of the individual person is protected by the affirmation that the principle of ultimate reality is a personal God."[37] Paradoxically, the personalism of Barth's sovereign God appears to depersonalize man.

The Janus-faced Character of Divine Personality

"Personality" is a notoriously elastic term. No dictionary definition will help us determine how it is being used. A personal God is normally associated with a moral God, one disposed to act in accordance with commonly understood moral standards. This is the interpretation given by Aiken, which we discussed earlier. We would be well advised to follow the counsel of contemporary linguistic analysts and ask what "job" the term "personality" is meant to perform in theology. In the case of theologians such as Barth, the idea of divine personality turns into a morally neutral concept. In their theological writings, divine personality more often refers to a will which is decidedly not to be rationalized or moralized. To live over against a living personality means to subordinate our moral concepts to His supramoral will. No system, no moral or rational standards are applicable to His will. Such a supramoral conception of divine personality appears essential to personalistic theodicies. For with such an inscrutable divine personality one may never be quite sure of the meaning of our moral predicates when applied to God. Faith in God is freed from an understanding of His moral character. Following Barth, to acknowledge God as person means to accept Him as He is; however He appears, He is to be experienced, not defined. The character of that experience, however, is unpredictable. What then does it mean to ascribe personality to God? Does "personality" ascribed to God refer to a supreme, self-subsistent, most perfectly intelligent being (Aquinas), or does it include a capacity to feel joy and suffering, an achievement born through conflict (Berdyaev)? Does it entail a willingness and capacity to relate to others (Brightman), or does it imply God's moral responsibility or confer obligations upon Him?

"Personality" is an ascriptive term. When it is applied to a supersensible being not subject to empirical observation, the intent and extent of the ascription are undetermined. The issue is not resolvable by consulting lexicon or scriptures. Verses may be cited, as we have done, to support a humanly comprehensible moral understanding of personality, and yet others may be quoted to sustain a supramoral interpretation. The name "person" as applied to God is not found in the Bible. We gain familiarity with the notion of a personal God indirectly through biblical and liturgical idioms which refer to God as "shepherd," "father," "ruler," "king," "judge." But precisely what moral character these terms suggest is left unclear.

When referring to God "personality" is not a predicate among predicates. It functions much like that logically odd term "existence"; a term to which linguistic analysts deny the status of predicate. "Existence" is not a quality or property of a subject but informs us that whatever concept is under discussion applies to something. Similarly, to speak of God's personality is to be advised that whatever attribute is under discussion refers to the subject. It refers to a unique "I," to a something or someone I know not what. It tells us that the subject is not an object, not an accessible essence, not approachable through an apprehension of general predicates.

Most personalistic theologians use personality to defend that absolute independence of God. In their theodicies its use effectively vitiates the very ground upon which the Jobian complaint is founded. For them personality as a divine predicate is as morally neutral a term as "holiness." Walter Eichrodt, in his discussion of the original biblical concept of holiness, tells us that holiness "resides not in the elevated moral standards, but in *the personal quality* of the God to which it refers."[38] Noteworthy in Eichrodt's analysis is his use of God's "personal" quality to characterize the amorality of holiness. To inquire into the ethical content of holiness is therefore to "ask the wrong question." It is, however, equally clear to Eichrodt that the later biblical tradition, preeminently through the prophets, transformed the supramoral meaning of holiness. The moral element "permeated the language of holiness even more strongly when the perfect fulfillment of social obligations came to be understood as the conduct truly in keeping with the divine holiness; and to such conduct the actual term holy was now applied."[39] Yehezkel Kaufmann, among other scholars, senses the tension between "religious" and "moral" demands in characterizing the nature of God. Within the Bible, one may observe the moral ideal, which sets limits upon the ways of God, as opposed to the religious ideal, which subjects all things and events to divine control without any restrictions. Kaufmann speaks of a "primary non-moral or supramoral element in monotheistic faith: the will and command of God is absolutely good."[40] The will of the sovereign personality is good by virtue of its origin, not by virtue of its content or consequence. Barth's use of "personality" in his theodicy, we suggest, tends toward an earlier supramoral, priestly understanding of holiness. In this reversion he has managed to shake loose the later religious association of morality with divine personality.

Between Man and Man

With Barth's use of "personality," man's ethical judgment is suspended. For Barth, "personalness" means being the subject "not only in the logical sense but also in the ethical sense."[41] Following Barth, we know, in some weak sense of the term "know," that the subject personality has qualities, but their signification eludes us. The epistemological and axiological distance between man and God is reflected in the absolute qualitative difference of the predicates when ascribed to each. God's goodness is not man's. Man is confronted with a hard disjunctive.

> Either we hear it as the command of His goodness (even though it is a command to shoot) or we do not hear it at all (even though it commissions us to preach). Either we obey it in the unity which it is always and everywhere true and valid . . . or we do not obey it. Either we love or we do not love. We are grateful or ungrateful.[42]

Faith and morality are thus disjoined. Man must choose between masters. Allegiance either to personality or to morality. Barth calls for man's total allegiance to the divine Ego whose commands will not be deciphered through the moral predicates assigned to Him. The results are clear. The moral predicates have been severed from the subject. Subject and predicates stand over against each other. Faith and morality stand in opposition.

What implication does the advocated subordination of man's moral judgment to the will of the determining subject hold beyond the arena of divine-human relationships? We have noted Barth's uncompromising insistence that man has "no normative conception of goodness, truth, right, love, salvation, well-being or peace with which to encounter God, to consider Him, to accept or reject Him, to wrestle with Him, to grasp or evade Him, to take up His cause or to argue with Him."[43] If it is faith in His personality not in morality which guides our relationship to God, is there another criterion outside obedience to His absolute word which may inform our relationship to man? We are reminded over and again that it is the existence of the Commander not the quality of the command that justifies our obedience. That command is not restricted to worship, nor is it abstract. The command is concrete, specific, one in form and in content, and its legitimation derives from its origination in the divine "I".[44] Man can appeal to no external referent for moral guidance. He can consult no lexicon of objective meaning; he can appeal neither to reason nor to conscience.

Faithful relationships with the single subject must prepare man not merely to transcend but even to oppose the humanly ethical domain. Given such a conception of divine personality, we are confronted with the possibility that the knight of faith may be commanded to "give his love to his neighbor the opposite expression to that which, ethically speaking, is required by duty."[45] The demands of the sovereign personality, Kierkegaard reminds us, are "capable of transforming a murder into a holy act well pleasing to God," as is indeed celebrated in the near-sacrifice of Isaac. What act may not be self-authenticated on the authority of the divine personality once the moral qualities of God are held to be incomprehensible to man? Once a radical qualitative difference between human and divine moral qualities is admitted, moral anarchy is let loose.

Mill's objection is particularly pertinent to our discussion.

> If I know nothing about what the attribute is, I cannot tell that it is a proper object of veneration. To say that God's goodness may be different in kind from man's goodness, what is it but saying, with a slight change of phraseology, that God may possibly not be good?[46]

We side with Mill in holding that trust in revelation presupposes the conviction that God's moral attributes are the same, in all but degree, with the best of man's moral attributes. Barth's alternative presents us with a theological cult of personality which is far from morally innocuous. Feuerbach's observation may be applied to Barth's use of "personality":

> Where the being is distinguished from love arises arbitrariness. Love acts from necessity, personality from will . . . . The highest worship of God as personal being is therefore the worship of God as an absolutely unlimited arbitrary being.[47]

Martin Buber: Evil and the Dialogic Principle

Martin Buber's celebrated characterization of man's two primary attitudes and relations, I-Thou and I-It, is essential to an appreciation of his view of evil. Through his perception of this *Urzweiheit*, Buber comes to his understanding of the duality of good and evil.

Through the I-It mode of being, man orients himself to the world and to himself as object. The "other" is seen either objectively or subjectively; analyzed as a categorizable entity or experienced in terms of personal "feelings." In either case, existence is dichotomized into subject and object. The "other" may be a tree or a horse, man or God. The I-It relation reduces the "other" to an observable, manipulable, predictable thing which is experienced and used. Love turns to possession, faith to security. No mutuality, no surprise is allowed to enter the mediated relationship. One cannot do without such relationships in the world. There are pragmatic needs and scientific goals which require order, precision, confirmability. But to live with such a mode of being alone is to deny oneself real living in meeting.

There is a relationship which man enters into with his whole being. The I-It relationship can never be entered into with one's undivided soul. It is the essential character of wholeness more than any other which distinguishes the I-Thou relationship from that of the I-It. Wholeness means that the other is approached without reservation, without holding back anything of one's entire being. It means that the other is accepted fully for what he is without any intention to use or transform him. The other is wholly free, wholly its own. The "I" is open to the uniqueness of the other and cannot anticipate what may emerge out of the direct meeting. What happens in such encounters is not reducible to the feelings of either "subject," nor is it reducible to the elements of either "object." The feelings or facts of an I-Thou relationship do not lend themselves to the familiar bifurcations of "inner" and "outer," subject and object, feelings and reason. They point to the hyphen of *das Zwischenmenschliche,* to the sphere of "betweenness" which bridges the separation of I and Thou. The unrehearsed meeting transforms one's life. What emerges from such a dialogue cannot be planned or reduced to a formula without turning it into a monologue.

Buber's dialogic principle is ontological in that it deals with man's relationship with being; and existential insofar as the principle is realized in the sphere of the existence of the person. Above all, the dialogical principle challenges any self-sufficient explanation which excludes the essential presence of the other. The genuine relationship Buber describes is "exclusive" in the sense that it fills our lives so that "all else lives in its light."[48] The other, met with wholeness, may reside in the sphere of nature, in the life with man, or with "spiritual beings."[49]

Only with the Eternal Thou is the relationship described as being both unconditionally exclusive and unconditionally inclusive.[50] Through this absolute relation with God nothing remains isolated, unrelated. But even at the height of relational intensity with the Eternal Thou, Buber is adamant in preserving the inviolable individuality of both bearers of the relation. Where the "I" in ecstasy is melted into the "Thou," there the dialogue disintegrates. Where the "Thou" is identified with the "I", there monologue reigns beneath the dialogic mask. Absorption or identification destroys the mutuality of genuine dialogue. For there to be nearness between man and the other, there must be distance. As one of the Hasidic masters whom Buber cites explains to his disciples: "If I am I because I am I, and you are you because you are you, then I am I and you are you. But if I am I because you are you, and you are you because I am I, then I am not I and you are not you."

Buber's philosophic orientation is particularly sensitive to the polarities of human existence and manifest in the two-fold attitude of man. His description of the human-divine relationships partakes of that pervasive sense of duality in unity which permeates his writings. God is the "wholly other" and yet just as much the "wholly same." "Of course, He is the *Mysterium Tremendum* that appears and overthrows; but He is also the mystery of the self-evident, nearer to me than my I."[51] Of course, man needs God. But God, "in the fullness of His reality," needs man. He who says "Thy will be done" may say no more, but truth adds for him "through me whom Thou needest."[52] God thus responds to man's dealings with the beings and things of the universe by pouring His divinity into all of nature. In this sense, it is man who "turns the world into a sacrament."[53]

What is required of man is his responsiveness to the call of the other. To be fully human man must make decisions. Authentic relationships demand decisions which are made with "all thy heart, with all thy soul and with all thy might." Good is defined by Buber in terms of decision and direction. Evil is equated with the decisionless, with the "aimless whirl of human potentialities."[54] Buber's definition of evil makes it privative. It refers to the lack of direction, the absence of personal wholeness, the failure to make a decision. Evil breeds on half-heartedness. It is manifest in one's halfway existence. Unwhole we are inclined to the unholy.

Buber's ideal of wholeness commits him to the extravagant claim that evil cannot be done with one's whole being.[55] When we hate, it is only with a part of us; and what we hate is only a part of the other. Through wholeness, evil can be turned to the service of God. With wholeness, we can learn to unite the parts and learn how to forgive the other.

There is risk in entering a dialogic relationship and risk in making decisions. One does not know beforehand what will happen in the encounter, and engaging the other with one's whole being renders one vulnerable to the other. There is no ethical system at hand to make one's decision safe and secure. It is once more to wholeness that Buber appeals as the "inward source" which may authenticate our decision. We may find confidence in "that we speak the true Thou only with the whole soul, where the stubborn contradiction no longer lurks in the corners."[56]

All the diverse decisions we are called upon to make are united by one direction taken by the unified soul. That direction may be apprehended as the movement toward becoming what we are uniquely intended to become.[57] Properly understood, the direction of I-Thou self-fulfillment expresses the direction toward God.

Buber has described his philosophic standpoint as "the narrow ridge." In his treatment of evil and his justifications of God's role in history, the precariousness of his stance becomes ever more apparent. His image of wholeness dominates his theological efforts to hold together God's nearness and His otherness, man's dependence and his freedom, his intimacy and fear of the Eternal Thou. Buber would, as it were, hold on to both sides of the cord which binds man to God in reciprocal relationship. In his portrayal of the reciprocity and interdependence of human and divine relationships, he has raised high expectations in man. With the advent of evil the dignity of the I and the closeness to the Thou are severely tested. Only the shock of evil throws Buber back into the arms of paradox so that his polarities may not be torn loose from their unifying source.

The Broken Dialogue

No contemporary religious philosopher has more deliberately stressed the centrality of the dialogic relationship between heaven and earth than Martin Buber. Man is created by God with an autonomy enabling him to "stand over against God."[58] Freedom and spontaneity characterize the independence of man in his engagement with the personal God. Israel knows the attributes of God in a manner sufficient to follow His way and to imitate Him.

But it is precisely that trusting personal intimacy and its dialogic presuppositions which are shaken by the Holocaust. The call and response between the above and the below which Buber describes as the biblical view of existence are blocked by a wall of terror. Job's cry escapes from the earth beneath which tradition has thought it buried:

> . . . how is a life with God still possible in a time in which there is an Oswiecim? The estrangement has become too cruel, the hiddenness too deep. One can still "believe" in the God who allowed these things to happen, but can one still speak to Him? Can one still as an individual and as a people, enter at all into a dialogic relationship with Him? Can one still call to Him? Dare we recommend to the survivors of Oswiecim, the Job of the gas chambers: "Call to Him for He is kind, for His mercy endureth forever"?[59]

The silence of a living God is more appalling than the apostasy which announces His demise. For the man of faith the gnawing doubt does not question that He lives but whether He cares; and if He cares, whether He cares enough to act.

Buber's response to his own grieving question is enigmatic. In the place of explanation, Buber can only offer expectation. We are counseled to wait for the reappearance of the hiding God. "Though His coming appearance resembles no other one, we shall recognize again our cruel and merciful God."[60]

The last is a sentence laden with ambiguity. How can we recognize His coming when it resembles no other one? Does the strangeness of His future advent suggest that Auschwitz marks a discontinuity of faith? Does the paradoxical conjunction "cruel and merciful" signify the breakdown of the intelligible moral syntax so crucial for dialogic communication? We must look elsewhere in Buber's writings to understand the implications of this odd conjunction of moral contraries.

In an important essay Buber contrasts personalistic faith, "the love of God," with the philosopher's conception, "the idea of deity."[61] Buber here refers to the Neo-Kantian philosopher Hermann Cohen, who identifies God with the moral ideal. Such identification, Buber warns, is destined to end in the breakdown of faith. The tragic contradictions between the moral ideal and the conduct of history can lead only to personal despair. More than principle, more than the archetype of the ideal, the living God is personality. More than personality, God is "absolute personality."[62]

This qualification of personality which Buber introduces is fully intended. He is aware of the paradoxical character of the phrase. The substantive concept "personality" combines with the adjective "absolute" in order "to contradict its normal concept."[63] For personality is too bound by moral associations to prevent Jobian disillusionment with God. An absolute, on the other hand, is unconditional, unlimited by standards or ideals, unrelated to and unbound by any other being. As such the absolute personality transcends the moral ideal. God is, as it were, the good beyond the good. So Buber insists that "the unity of God is not the good; it is the supergood."[64] Such a God must be accepted and loved "in His deepest concealment."[65] All the ingredients for a personalistic theodicy are at hand. A supragood absolute personality will produce no Jobian discontent. Job will accept every moral incongruity of life without resentment. He who

> begins to provide himself with a comprehensible God, constructed thus and not otherwise, runs the risk of having to despair of God in view of the actualities of history and life, or falling into inner falsehood. Only through the fear of God does man enter so deep into the love of God that he cannot be cast out of it.[66]

There is pragmatic wisdom in Buber's radicalization of an earlier understanding of the I-Thou relationship. Expecting nothing or anything of God, Job cannot be disappointed. All anticipations of God's goodness derive from Job's ignorant conceits, from the alleged unity of goodness which forms the moral ideal of God.

Through his notion of God as absolute personality Buber has removed the ground from under the feet of the old Job. We are tempted to ask wherein such a faith in a suprapersonal, supramoral God differs from a religious masochism which finds love in the signs of indifference or hostility? Faith in an incomprehensible supergood personality may prevent disillusionment, but it is a resolution as desperate as plucking out one's eyes to forestall the possible loss of vision.

Buber has provided costly safeguards against Jobian despair. The paradoxes which unite absoluteness with personality and the good with the supergood are consistent with the paradox of his "merciful and cruel God." It cannot be denied, however, that the earlier intimacy, trust, and reciprocity characterized by Buber's I-Thou relationship are no longer the same. Job has been intimidated by the absolute personality. How can he protest, in the manner which Buber describes as his legitimate struggle, against the "God-given" verdict of history which issues in evil?[67]. Having shattered the idols of a humanly comprehensible God, Buber, it would appear to us, has lost the reason to encourage Job's rebellion. And yet, Buber writes:

> My father Job (no Israelite, it seems and yet my father) protests and trusts in one; we come to feel that to love his own fate remains alien to him to the end, and God encourages him not to love it. He stands in an unsurpassably awesome dialogue; but God does not deny himself to him as a partner in dialogue.[68]

Nor is it clear what remains of Buber's personal God after his qualifications have been made. On the one hand, we cannot reduce God's absoluteness to a personality. In addressing God as person "we are making no statement about the absolute which reduces it to the personal."[69] Yet we are allowed by God, "so to speak," to experience Him as person.[70] We are given permission to speak and believe that the absolute becomes a person "because in our human mode of existence the only reciprocal relation with us that exists is a personal one."[71] There is a marked unclarity here. Is the personalistic language allowed as an accommodation to man's conceptual limitations in describing his relationship to the absolute? Or does it affirm an independent ontologic status of personality to God? Buber, in his important postscript to the second edition of *I and Thou*, argues for the description of God as a Person.[72] God's personality makes it possible for man to enter into a relationship of mutuality with the Eternal Thou. The existence of this mutuality between God and man cannot be proved but can be testified to by witnesses who have experienced dialogic relationship. Does, however, the personal relationship experienced by man with the other testify to the other as a "Person God"?[73] The grounds for such a claim are not different from those which, for Buber, establish the "thou-ness" of a tree or horse. We recall that, for Buber, it can happen through "will and grace" that man can become bound up in a relation to a tree which is mutual.[74] The wholeness and unity of the tree is said to disclose itself "to the glance of one who says Thou."[75] He recalls that the horse he stroked as a child "placed itself elementally in the relation of *Thou* and *Thou* with me."[76]

Buber, we contend, confuses the *reality of a personal experience* with the *experience of a real person*. The intensity of a relationship which affects me personally is neither proof nor witness to the personality of the other. The fact that our intentions toward others may alter our personal feeling and comprehension *of them* in no way legitimates the ascription of the properties of personality, feeling, and intelligence *to them*. To ascribe personality to the other and claim a relationship of mutuality with the other on grounds of truly intense, personal experience is logically illicit and morally open to all kinds of dangers. We sense that Buber's *als ob* sanction to speak of God as person betrays his own unresolved ambiguity in this matter.

Ethical Decision and Absolute Personality

There are other complications in speaking of God as person, particularly in the realm of moral decision. There is a price to be paid for abandoning morally comprehensible ideals to the personal or suprapersonal absolute. There is equally a price to be paid for holding firm to moral principles and to the right to live according to their intelligibility. The first decision affects our ethics, the other our theology.

Relationships between man and the absolute personality at times eventuate in a command to act. But Buber is unhappy with the fideist response of the knight of faith who suspends the ethical and submits to the imperatives of the supramoral divine person. He is troubled by the sinister ventriloquism of the Moloch of our times, which commands in God's name.[77] Unable to accept Kierkegaard's teleological suspension of the ethical, Buber would have us treat Abraham and his era as exceptional. It is not at all easy for us to understand why Buber thinks he can safely assign the Abraham-Isaac event to the past, or to accept his confidence that "Abraham, to be sure, could not confuse with another the voice which once made him leave his homeland and which he at that time recognized as the voice of God without the speaker saying to him who he was."[78] From the rest of us, in our confused age, God demands nothing more than justice and love, "not much more than the fundamental ethical."[79] Here Buber's ethics of belief turns him to the humanly comprehensible moral connotation of goodness.

Yet Buber's moral pragmatism cannot be so readily squared with his conviction that there can be no ethical criterion to be consulted when it is God's will which is to be fulfilled. As Buber tells us, "He who really believes in God cannot acknowledge *any other court* above his."[80] To believe in the God above the good is to subordinate the fundamental ethical to the absolute person. Buber's oscillation and paradoxical language betray his torn commitments to both a moral and supramoral idea of divine personality. Haunted by the shades of Auschwitz, Buber feels compelled to hide the moral ideal behind the hidden God of Absolute Personality. We are not persuaded that the "cruel and merciful God" is responsive to the Jobian outcry. Buber contends that the philosopher's idea of the absolute dissolves "at the point where the absolute is loved."[81] It seems to us that his own idea of the divine personality dissolves at the point where it is no longer lovable, at the point where Auschwitz appears.

The Comprehensibility of God

The personalistic theodicies of Barth and Buber are curiously allied with the metaphysical theodicies in de facto abandoning the moral connotation of goodness when ascribed to God. However else they differ, in their deflection of the moral ideal and the deflation of man's capacity to know the moral attributes of God, metaphysical and personalistic theodicies are united. In common, traditional theodicies tend sooner or later to fall upon the incomprehensibility of God as their ultimate argument. The theological rationalist Maimonides insists upon a predicate agnosticism. "It cannot be said . . . that His existence is only more stable, His life more permanent, His wisdom more perfect and His will more general than ours."[82] There is no qualitative similarity between His virtues and ours. "Anything predicated of God is totally different from our attributes."[83] All terms such as "justice," "love," "goodness" when applied to both God and man are homonymous.

Barth typically interprets the Psalmist's declaration of the infinite trustworthiness and righteousness of God as expressing "the incomprehensibility of His goodness and faithfulness."[84] The verse from Isaiah 55 is cited to evidence the absolute, qualitatively different attributes of God and man. "For my thoughts are not your thoughts, neither are your ways My ways, saith the Lord."[85]

But even on exegetical grounds, such theological interpretations, which make of these statements assertions of the inscrutability and wholly other character of the divine attributes, may be shown to err. The context of the oft-cited verse reveals no such intention. The succeeding verse explains its proper context.

> For as the rain cometh down and the snow from heaven,
> And returneth not thither,
> Except it water the earth,
> And make it bring forth and bud,
> And give seed to the sower and bread to the eater;
> So shall My word be that goeth forth out of My mouth:
> It shall not return unto Me void
> Except it accomplish that which I please,
> And make the thing whereto I sent it prosper.[86]

The prophet contrasts the efficacy and trustworthiness of God's ways with the impotence and backsliding of the faithless. God's thoughts and ways are "more" reliable, "more" just; but for all the difference in degree, they are not qualitatively "other" than the same attributes of goodness and faithfulness which apply to man. God is not man, because He restrains the fierceness of His anger and exercises His compassion.[87] The very call for man to imitate God's ways presupposes a qualitative continuity between divine and human moral virtues. The metaphysical attributes of omnipotence, eternity, and infinity are not emulable and may not be understood, but *imitatio dei* requires an understanding of His moral qualities.

Ironically, as Mill noted, theologians seem interested in restricting man's ability to comprehend God's powers only with regard to those which describe His moral qualities. "We are never told that God's omnipotence must not be supposed to mean an infinite degree of the power we know in man and nature, and that perhaps it does not mean that he is able to kill us, or consign us to eternal flames."[88] Why then is the human signification of metaphysical powers justifiable while that of the moral powers is denied? We suggest that one major motivation for such moral-predicate agnosticism is to deny the legitimacy of any moral critique of God. The "supra" prefixes which theologians attach to His goodness, and the mystery of His personality which they accentuate, manage to exclude the moral ideal of divine perfection from religious belief. It is a costly strategy for religion. *Quod supra nos, nihil ad nos*; what is beyond us is nothing to us. The *argumentum ad ignorantiam* of theodicy, however sophisticated, blunts the moral relationship between God and man predicated upon a common understanding of goodness. It denies a knowledge without which Paul could not contend, "For what can be shown about God is plain to them, because God has shown it to them."[89]

John Hick: the Personal God of Infinite Love

"A theology cannot go unchallenged when it is repugnant to the moral sense that has been formed by the religious realities upon which their theology itself professes to be based."[90] A number of contemporary theologians are sensitive to the dismissal of the moral nerve by traditional theodicies of theism. They attempt a theodicy whose metaphysics is neither transmoral, transhuman, nor aesthetic. The structure of the universe accommodates the human personality and the moral design of the Creator. The physical order of the universe provides the most suitable setting for the human theater of moral choice.

John Hick has presented the most thorough contemporary analysis of the problem of evil, along with his own moral theodicy.[91] He favors the Irenaean as opposed to the Augustinian way of thinking about human suffering and God's providential designs. Without denying the value of the universe independent of man, the Irenaean emphasis is upon a God-fashioned universe which is the most fitting environment for man's moral and religious maturation. "For if God is the Personal Infinite, man alone among God's creatures is, so far as we know, capable of personal relationship with Him."[92] Man is singled out and given a special place in the universe. The good in the subhuman realm is to be evaluated in terms of its contribution to the good in the human realm.

To interpret the biblical account of Adam's fall without Augustinian editing, Hick contends, would portray man not as cast down from the high rung of original perfection. Man's fallenness refers to his status as an "imago" of God contrasted with his ideal status as "likeness" of God. It points to his immaturity, not to his brokenness. Adam is immersed in a natural world, surrounded by technical wisdom, seduced by the Serpent, the first scientist and naturalist on earth. Adam's absorption in the material world blinds him to the vision of God. This alienation is "virtually inevitable," the price which finitude pays for freedom. We have seen in our discussion of Paul Tillich a similar understanding of fallenness as separation, "the point at which creation and the fall coincide." For Reinhold Niebuhr man's sin is also treated as inevitable, "yet without escaping responsibility of his sin." William Temple likewise evaluates the self-centeredness of finite and autonomous man as "too probable not to happen."[93] There is a blessed paradox in man's creaturely freedom. Separation from God is the requisite for coming to union with Him. The very rebellion of man against God will turn out to be a happy fault. The epistemic distance between God and man, which makes it virtually inevitable that man ignore God, is transmuted into a gift. For "man can be truly for God only if he is morally independent of Him, and he can be thus independent only by being first *against* Him."[94] There is no shortcut to faith born of struggle against sin. The love of God cannot be coerced by Him. It must be earned by man's struggle in the condition of freedom, and that struggle entails suffering. In the background of man's cognitive freedom and his own self-realization is the hidden God who awaits discovery by the human faith response.

The immaturity of man and the attending pains and sufferings are necessary elements in the ascension of the ladder to salvation. God has sprinkled the universe with sufficient precariousness to elicit the noblest human response. There is method in the madness of the universe. It is part of the "vale of soul-making" (Keats). Such a vantage point draws attention to the ambivalence of blessing and curse. Who has not observed the malediction in prosperity and the benediction in adversity? Dysteleological suffering often energizes man, who overcomes his passivity and insularity in struggling against his lot. A controlling, benevolent deity would infantilize man and lock him into the "imago" status. A world without pain would anesthetize existence and destroy the stimuli requisite for human culture and civilization.[95] A world in which the innocent were protected by divine intervention would entail supranatural control over physical laws, e.g., bullets melting into thin air, gravitational laws suspended. The result would be a world without consequences. Crimes would lose their meaning, virtues would be superfluous, and human beings robbed of moral growth. A one-to-one divine response to human need would yield a wooden, utilitarian piety. It would result in a flat universe, neither blameworthy nor praiseworthy. The irregularities of nature -- earthquake, hurricane, tornado -- leave destruction in their wake. But as Nels Ferré argues, disasters foster in man "a common dependence on something beyond us, the need to cooperate with each other, and a feeling of constant insecurity on the plane of human power, goodness and wisdom."[96] Natural evil humbles man, protects him from the sin of self-sufficient finitude, evokes in him scientific curiosity and the development of technological control over the threatening forces of nature.[97] Sickness and death are God's shock treatment whereby man is delivered from false securities and acquiescent behavior.

Of what value is the suffering of innocence in the course of the exercise of moral evil? We are members of one human family, and such unity means that the sin of one man affects us all. Our life is corporate, and we share in common both the good and the evil of others.[98] Undeserved human suffering evokes the qualities of sympathy, sacrifice, and organized relief. The very innocence of human suffering gives rise to compassion.[99] Without *Leid* there would be no *Mitleid*. Certainly, even granting some of the benevolent consequences of physical and moral evil, such suffering appears excessive. Could not the pain and anguish be reduced without eliminating the virtues of struggle, compassion, mutual aid? Would a million souls less than the 11 million slaughtered in the Holocaust have diminished the sympathy of the world? Need the rains turn into hurricanes, the winds into tornadoes, to make their point? To these and other acknowledged problems of evil, Hick responds by summoning the majesty of mystery. Not knowing how to answer the problem of disproportionate and undeserved suffering leads us to faith beyond knowledge. The very irrationality and lack of ethical meaning of haphazard and excessive suffering "contribute to the character of the world as a place in which true human goodness can occur and in which loving sympathy and compassionate self-sacrifice can take place."[100] The very failure to answer the hardest questions of evil points to the positive value of mystery. Hick concludes his theodicy with an eschatological resolution. The ultimate life of man and the ultimate theodicy lie in the future, in the blissful happiness of the Kingdom of God. Contrary to the bookkeeping doctrine of divine compensation proportionate to the suffering endured, Hick's eschatological theodicy leads to an unending and unlimited enjoyment of a common good for all. It is a theodicy which does not deny the reality of evil but which, like the medieval doctrine of *felix culpa* (the "happy fault"), defeats it and lifts it up to serve God's benevolent design.[101]

Critical Observations

One must acknowledge at the outset the moral centrality of Hick's approach. His theodicy centers upon moral personality rather than upon nature as a whole and upon ethical rather than aesthetic virtues. Its chief failure lies in the compatibility of its explanations with any set of possible conditions. What would it be to be presented with genuinely unjustified evil? Even admittedly irrational and ethically meaningless events are seen as instrumentally good, serving God's ultimate purpose. Hick's ultimate eschatological theodicy eliminates the possibility of genuine, radical evil. For the doctrine of divine resurrection and recreation of the human personality after death, every evil is seen as having played a part in the fulfillment of God's purpose and thereby has contributed to good. The very fall of humanity is an instrumental good. From the ultimate perspective, then, every evil is seen as such only from the narrow view of present experience. Used in the creation of infinite good, it loses the quality of evil. Stability or disequilibrium, harmony or disintegration, the truimph or failure of the righteous all turn out to be good in the end. Hick's theodicy lies safe in the arms of a grand *argumentum ad ignorantiam*. To know that an event is gratuitously evil one would have to possess complete knowledge of possible goods and their connection with evil. No theodicy claims such knowledge. Given the wide-open future and the limitless oscillations of good and evil, the claim that all events are ultimately good is not subject to disconfirmation. Under which conceivable conditions will such omni-compatible theodicies admit falsifiability?

Hick himself raises questions to which he can offer no better response than a pious shrug. While in his treatment of pain he argues for its biological function in offering warning signals, he knows of cases where pain has no useful warning function. Pain as an instrument of self-preservation is under normal circumstances and in general valuable, but there are more than a few cases where pain has no function and is excessive. The pain which comes only when the disease is far advanced and its warning unneeded, or in a primitive stage of history before the days of medicine and surgery, does more harm than good.

Moreover, the touted compensation of freedom for suffering seems hardly appropriate where pain and affliction destroy the very faculties indispensable for making free choice. The attack which paralyzes the brain allows no opportunity to learn from experience or exercise the will. The argued value of pain in strengthening the character and developing empathy ignores the suffering which crushes the spirit of man and embitters his view of life. Pain and suffering are morally neutral events. It is the interpretation of such events, not the events themselves, which serves the end of moral growth and sensitivity. If so, then at the very heart, suffering ought to be distributed with wiser parsimony. The intensity and quantity of suffering could readily be halved without reducing the lessons which may be derived from their experience.

The major assumption of such theodicies would indicate an overexalted valuation of freedom. Is the nonintervention of a father who sees his child running toward a bottomless pit morally justifiable on the grounds that the father means by his inaction to strengthen his child's autonomy? Is freedom of greater value to God than preventing the excruciating pain of a stricken child? Ivan Karamazov's outcry against the harmony of the heavens in the face of the torture of an innocent child is not muted by the praise of autonomy.

The nonintervention of God on the grounds that He chooses freedom for humanity appears strange in the writings of those who celebrate the wonders of God recorded in scripture. Was the miracle at the Red Sea no sign of God's love? Why is His repeated dramatic intrusion in the course of biblical history not evaluated as inimical to the freedom of man? Why are the miracles of the ten plagues considered signs of God's concern and not suspensions of natural law which frustrate human predictability and control? For biblically oriented writers of theodicy to explain the suffering of innocent bystanders because of the sin of others on the grounds that we are an interdependent human community is equally odd. Did not the prophet chastise those who proclaimed that "the fathers have eaten sour grapes and the children's teeth are set on edge"?[102] That God's concern extends even to the solitary sparrow and the innocent individual does not mean that to suffer unwillingly for the iniquities of another is basic to the biblical ethic.

Hick's trump card, the eschatological resolution of those inexplicable and excessive sufferings, makes man's evolutionary struggle a superfluous affair. After all, He who creates man with inevitable failings will ultimately redeem all, including those who fail to respond to the challenge. No personal life that is unperfected and no human sin will be left unredeemed. There is no ledger in heaven proportioning reward to injury, and there is no damnation in hell. God wins all men to Himself in faith and in love.

Such universal salvation appears overly indiscriminate. It expresses a generosity which blurs the distinction between aggressor and victim. In terms of reward and punishment, what differentiates the lot of the righteous from that of the wicked? All human beings, saints and villains, will be saved. The wicked may require more time to mature morally. This extension of time is granted them in an intermediate state in which the sanctifying process is completed. The intermediate state is, of course, no joy. Though the eternal suffering of hell is dismissed as cruel and unusual punishment, the purgatorial experiences of the intermediate state are "real and dreadful and rationally to be feared."[103] Yet, sooner or later, all is forgiven and forgotten. For if the memory of our anguish remains with us to the end, no posthumous heavenly joy can erase the scars of human suffering. Suffering passes but not the fact of having suffered. And if eschatological theodicy celebrates the happiness of heaven for all, and the memory of earthly pain is dimmed to the point of extinction, the monster and the saint are treated by God evenhandedly.

The seriousness of this life, the incentive for "soulmaking" and for transforming society, is diminished by the tales of eschatological redemption. The reality of evil, which Hick acknowledges, is less real in the face of his eschatological speculation wherein dysteleological suffering is transmuted by the promise of another life and another world. The human struggle and agony of the righteous appear gratuitous, and God appears as a benevolent spectator of a grim human sport.

Chapter 6
Toward a Predicate Theodicy

Not the attribute of divinity but the divinity of the attribute is the first truly divine being.

--Ludwig Feuerbach

The failure of theodicies is moral. Nietzsche summed up the resentment of the modern sensibility in rejecting the explanations and consolations of theodicy:

> To look upon nature as if it were proof of the goodness and care of a God; to interpret history in honor of a divine reason, as a constant testimony to a moral order in the world and a moral final purpose; to explain personal experiences as pious men have long enough explained them, as if everything were a dispensation or intimation of Providence, something planned and set on behalf of the salvation of the soul: all that is passed; it has conscience against it.[1]

The protestation registers more than negation. It defies more than it denies. To have "conscience against it" indicates a fidelity to moral principle which in turn carries the seeds of a credible theodicy.

We have argued that the God-idea of metaphysics is not the God-idea of personalism. After the work of their respective theodicies is done, neither resembles the God of morality. Such a judgment is reflected in Kant's assessment of the moral failure of all possible theodicies. Theodicies, Kant wrote, offer an "apology in which the defense is worse than the charge [and which] require no confutation, and may certainly be fully left to the detestation of everyone who has the least sense or spark of morality."[2]

The moral price of theodicy is grasped by Max Weber in his overview of the various types of theodicy. In common they all end up counseling the human being to adopt an attitude of "masochism."[3] In the last analysis, the individual is a cipher, guilty or not, whose wisest consolation is found in his surrender to "the ordering power of society." In the absorption of his self in the Other, he overcomes loneliness and meaninglessness. To belong to the holy "wholly other" may not promise happiness; but it does offer meaning. If he would salvage meaning from his personal holocaust, let him who suffers submit to God's meaning. For God, there is meaning in everything. For Him no evil remains evil. The sufferer transcends his burdens by placing them into the arms of the transcendent. Such "transcendentalization of God" further separates the ground of the victim's complaint from God. If evil points to fault it may be found in man's self-centeredness, in the magnification of his provincial sorrows, and in the abuse of his freedom. In this manner, the Jobian trial has shifted its venue from the justification of God to the accusation of man, from theodicy to anthropodicy.

The Predicateless Subject

Theodicies are not formed in a vacuum. They are wed to theologies, for better or for worse, and their vows are taken to support and protect them. The very grammar of theology frames the character of theodicy. Theological statements are traditionally expressed in terms of subject-predicate relations. However the idea of God is portrayed, whether as being, power, person, or process, it refers to a subject. The subject is the underlying entity, the substratum to which attributes are ascribed. The divine subject, as it were, supports and holds together the qualities. The subject alone is accepted as unqualifiedly real and objective. By contrast the predicates are nebulous figures forever being explained away as homonyms or negative attributes or hobbled analogies of human virtues or incomprehensible divine qualities. Sensitive to the charge of anthropomorphism, much of traditional theology spends its energy denying literal, positive, and univocal meaning to the predicates, and in the arguments of theodicy especially to the moral predicates of the divine subject. Thus a personalist theist such as Judah Halevi describes "creative," "negative," and "relative" attributes as accommodations to our finite understanding. "All these attributes neither touch on the divine essence, nor do they assume a multiplicity."[4] They are borrowed from the desire to give reverence to Him, or used to emphasize the inapplicability of positive attributes to God, or to contrast His virtue with others. We may say that the rays of the light are inseparable from the sun, although we know it is not so. We may say that the predicates are inseparable from the essence of God, though we know it is not so. "The sun is uniform; but the bodies receiving its light react in different ways."[5] The attributes of the divine subject are ambiguously reflected in the predicates.

For Maimonides, predicates such as "goodness," "life," and "power" when applied to God are homonymous, veritable puns. They are properly understood as negations, signifying that God is not evil, not lifeless, and not powerless. Even those biblical predicates which refer to His relations with creation tell us nothing positive about God's attributes. God performs actions which may appear similar to ours. But the similarity of effect does not warrant imputing motivation or disposition to God. The result of an act of God may suggest to us that He is angry, but such an inference stems from erroneous anthropathetic thinking.[6] We can say only that God is an incomparable being to whom no predicates are properly applicable.[7] We know only the subject; only that He exists.

Aquinas does admit positive predications of God, "although they fall short of representing Him."[8] He favors the analogy of proportionality, which applies predicates of perfection according to the nature of the analogates. But the limitation of such analogical predication is obvious. How can we meaningfully apply a predicate of perfection in accordance with God's nature when we know nothing of His preeminent nature except that it is infinitely different from any other? Without knowledge of the true dignity of the transcendent analogue, how can we determine the proper mode of signification?[9] Indeed, one of Aquinas's interpreters, F. C. Copleston, admits to a certain agnosticism in Thomas's account of our natural knowledge of divine nature.[10] No adequate description of what is objectively signified by a predicate of God, then, can be given. We know *quod est*, that God is. "He who is" is commended by Aquinas as the most appropriate name of God because of its indeterminateness. It determines no mode of being but names "the infinite ocean of substance."[11]

Classical theology generally leaves us with a supersensible subject, necessary, independent, eternal. We know that the subject exists and that its essence is to exist. We know that the subject is the Cause of all causes and excels all things caused by it. By contrast, the predicates hang in its shadows.

It is not much different with personalistic theologies, which reject the negative theology of the classic philosophers. Initially, the personalized God promises a more full-blooded subject. But as we have observed in our discussion of Barth and Buber, the personality of God takes on a suprapersonal character. Functionally, it is often used to deny the propriety of applying predicates to His person. We are left, in effect, with a predicateless ultrapersonal subject. The infinite qualitative difference between the divine and human predicates will prevent any humanly comprehensible employment of the predicate of God. Latin-writing theologians used *persona* as a term equivalent to the Greek *hypostasis*, a "standing under" or "below," and this subsequently was translated into Latin as *substantia*.[12] The equivalence of personality and substance portends the functional sameness of "personality" and "being." Both have been used to refer to the underlying divine subject which eclipses the predicates.

Subject Theodicy

Theodicies follow suit. Under the impact of the problem of evil, the role of the subject becomes totally dominant. For the basis of the challenge of evil depends upon the positive meaning of the predicates. The challenge is grounded in the comprehensible moral predicates of "goodness," "justice," "mercy" which are ascribed to God. The character of the subject's will and acts is attacked on the basis of the meaning of the moral predicates. If the predicates are equivocal half-truths inapplicable to the description of God's nature, the very foundation of the assault is loosened. The writers of theodicy have inherited a subject-dominated theology, and it is the subject which they are committed to defend. Destroy the legitimacy of the predicate and the subject is armed with invulnerability. Question the positive meaning of the moral predicates and the Jobian sword is broken. To protect the subject, the moral predicates must be qualified out of their normal connotation.

In Barth's sharp enunciation we have seen the critical role which the subject plays in so many arguments of theodicy. "Strictly speaking, there is no divine predicate, no idea of God which can have as its special content *what* God is. There is strictly speaking only the Divine Subject as such and in Him the fitness of His divine predicates."[13] There is a boldness in Barth's statement which blows away the dust that covers much of the strategy of traditional theodicy. The subject simply cannot be measured by its ascribed predicates. The two are incommensurable. They are severed de facto in theodicy. The subject refers to a "who," the predicates to a "what." The subject of theology is "He who is." For Barth and many others, "what" He is suggests an irreverent and impossible quest.

The subject, "He who is," need not square His actions with any set of allegedly comprehensible predicates. "Who" dominates "what" and, in the last analysis, remains the sole answer to the question, "Why did it happen?" However the theodicies seek to harmonize God's ways with His goodness, they will ultimately be forced back to the inscrutable will of the subject. God's goodness flows from His personality, not from the attributes men dare think they can properly ascribe to Him. No matter how the God-idea and moral attributes may be initially formulated as good and caring, in the wake of the storm which evil stirs up, theodicies retreat to the mysterious and supramoral subject. In the case of metaphysical theology, however rational the explanation of God's way in the face of evil, the normal moral connotation of God and its normal human reference are abandoned. To what end the turmoil and suffering of His creation? To what purpose the creation of man and the limitations placed upon him? As Maimonides put it, "We must in continuing the inquiry as to the purpose of creation at last arrive at the answer. It was the will of God or His wisdom that decreed it; and this is the correct answer."

The Splitting of Subject and Predicate

No one has traced the twists and turns which eventuate in the opposition of subject and predicate more closely than that "keen-eyed spy of theology" Ludwig Feuerbach. He argued, to our mind compellingly, that before religion aged into rationalized theology, it had drawn a quantitative distinction between the divine and human predicates.[15] God's predicates were "more than" those ascribed to man. God was more reliable, more just, more compassionate than man. No one could disguise the quantitative disparity. Qualitatively, however, the moral attributes belonged within the same spectrum. The covenant of reciprocity, the ideal of *imitatio dei,* presupposed a qualitative sameness of the moral terms. The distance between God and man is admittedly enormous, but even so the distinction is a matter of degree, not of kind. If, however, the moral predicates mean one thing when applied to human beings and something incomprehensibly other when ascribed to God, no ethical universe of discourse can be said to exist. Not only is a critique of God's ways impossible, but a critique of man's conduct is similarly jeopardized. From the vantage point of a supramoral God, who knows whether our moral judgments of our society correspond to His moral criteria? In the theological conversion of "more than" to "other than" an unbridgeable chasm is formed. This is the work of theology and theodicy. Biblical religion, in contrast to theology, opposes the rupture. "I have not spoken in secret, in a place of the land of darkness; I said not unto the seed of Jacob: 'Seek ye Me in vain.' I the Lord speak righteousness. I declare things that are right."[16]

The man of biblical faith knows *what* God is. The theologian knows only *that* He is. The latter has faith in the subject. But faith in the subject is not a moral but a personal faith. Such a faith does not love the subject because He is lovable but because He is sovereign. Is it then to the subject or to the moral predicates that the man of faith owes his supreme loyalty? Is faith allegiance to the "who" or to the "what" of divinity? If a conflict between the mandates of morality and the mandates of His personal sovereignty arises, which ought man to follow? Faith, as Barth and Kierkegaard understood it, calls for unconditional fidelity to the unconditioned subject. They may hold extreme positions, but they indicate some of the consequences flowing from a subject-oriented theology. Following the vertical split between subject and moral predicate, faith and morality are bifurcated into opposing claims. For those whose faith is in the subject alone, morality depends upon the commands imposed by the sovereign subject. No set of predicates can evaluate the morality of His imperatives.

Critics of such a view conclude that given a morally predicateless subject, all ethical definitions vanish.[17] While Karamazov argued that if there is no God all is permitted, it may be countered that with a God emptied of morally comprehensible predicates, all things may be divinely sanctioned. If the ground of morality depends upon faith in an inscrutable subject who may permit tomorrow what He prohibits today -- and who would deny Him that freedom -- all may be permitted. Belief in the absolute freedom of God, which refuses to bind Him to moral constraints, loses its moral restraint upon the Torquemadas of history. Whether villains may be properly condemned depends not on belief in God's existence but upon the intelligibility of His moral character and dictates. Feuerbach reminds us that the Devil too believes in God's existence and His power. "Whether under this [subject] God thou conceivest a really divine being or a monster, a Nero or a Caligula, an image of thy passions, thy revenge or ambition, it is all one -- the main point is that thou be not an atheist."[18] Moral atheism, the denial of the moral predicates, and not subject atheism is the real threat to religious faith. The schism of subject and moral predicate presages the chasm between faith and morality and the alienation of man from God.

Toward A Predicate Theology

Is there an alternative to the inherited form of subject theology and subject theodicy? Can the moral ideal of divine perfection be conceptualized without its being devoured by an omnivorous subject? Is there another way to integrate the insights and values of metaphysical and personalistic theology without violating the moral dimension? In *The Essence of Christianity* Feuerbach boldly proposed "inverting the oracles of religion." While much of Feuerbach's Copernican revolution suffers from a far too simplistic reductionism, it contains perceptive insights which point the way toward a positive reconstruction of theology and theodicy. From his sharpest critic, Karl Barth, we may learn to value "the attitude of the anti-theologian Feuerbach [which] was more theological than that of many theologians."[19]

We consider Feuerbach's inversion proposal as a pedagogic and methodologic principle: ". . . that which in religion is the predicate we must make the subject, and that which in religion is a subject we must make a predicate."[20] The first shall become last and the last first. The predicates are no longer seen as qualities which derive their meaning from the subject. The predicates are now the proper subject of theology. They assume a new status. We look to them to understand the character of divinity.

The theological task changes accordingly. The aim is not to prove the existence of the subject but to demonstrate the reality of the predicates. For subject theology faith is belief in the subject and atheism is the denial of its existence. For predicate theology faith is belief in the reality of the predicates and atheism is their denial. The critical question for predicate theology is not "Do you believe that God is merciful, caring, peacemaking?" but "Do you believe that doing mercy, caring, making peace are godly?" The energy of theology would be directed not toward convincing men that a subject possesses certain qualities themselves. Following the inversionary proposal, the religious contention is not that a subject is in some sense good or loving or intelligent or creator but that the humanly comprehensible qualities of goodness, love, intelligence, and creativity are godly; that they themselves are worthy of adoration, cultivation, and emulation in the lives of the believers. In Feuerbach's formulation, "God does not love, He is himself love; He does not live, He is life; He is not just but justice itself; not a person, but personality itself."[21] What is important to note here is that the qualities do not derive their meaning and their worth from another realm of being. They are experienced and valued for themselves. They are not valued as appendages attached to a supersensible subject but are discovered in the course of man's transactions with his environment, human and nonhuman. They are not cast down from above or projected from below but revealed in the areas between persons and between persons and things. As we have seen, between man and the divine subject an unbridgeable qualitative gap exists. Between man and the divine predicates no such distance prevails. "It is not in heaven, that thou shouldest say, 'Who shall go up for us to heaven, and bring it down to us, that we may hear it and do it?' Neither is it beyond the sea, that thou shouldest say, 'Who shall go over the sea for us, and bring it unto us, that we may hear it and do it?' But the word is very nigh unto thee, in thy mouth and in thy heart, that thou mayest do it."[22]

The nearness is facilitated by the attention which predicate orientation cultivates. The very language which is used to formulate theological propositions and liturgy is biased toward the subject. We will have more to say about the relationship of syntax to theology. For the present, and by way of illustrating the contrast between the subject and predicate orientations, we turn to the language of traditional benedictions. The liturgical formulation which praises God for bringing forth bread from the earth is typically stated in the mode of subject theology. It centers upon a "who" or a Thou or a He through whose will and act the bread is presented. All praise is due to the subject. A predicate formulation, "that which brings forth bread from the earth," directs the worshipper's attention to the complexity of events, which elicits reverence and praise. What transactions bring forth the bread? We are drawn to acknowledge the givenness of earth and seed, water and sun, the human effort to prepare the soil, to weed and plough and plant, to harvest the field, to reap and winnow and grind the wheat, to knead and season the dough, to distribute bread for the sake of human life and health. The vertical image of subject theology has been horizontalized and its misplaced concreteness relocated. The activity is not projected onto a preexisting subject, but unfolded so that the relationships between human and nonhuman elements are revealed.

What is being proposed, of course, is not simply an inversion of the syntactical places of the subject and the predicate. The issue is not a matter of grammar. To replace the theological statement "God is good" with "goodness is God" simply substitutes an abstract for a proper noun. Far more is intended. The priority assigned to the predicate, which in subject theology lived in the shadow of the subject, implies a new mode of thinking about God and Godliness.

The project of predicate theology, which we briefly sketch in the following few sentences, will be detailed in the remainder of this chapter. To see God or godliness through the eyes of the predicates focuses upon the complex processes which disclose godly qualities, the proper objects of adoration and emulation. The God-terms of subject theology, which have been reified, enwrapped in noun substantives and located in an occult Power, are unravelled and demystified. The transactions between the self, individual and collective, and the environment, human and nonhuman, are revelatory. Qualities are discovered in doing, feeling, thinking, willing, prizing, and evaluating experience. They are, in large part, products of cumulative experience, inherited from prior generations of individual and collective experience. They are added to and refined through our own experiences and evaluations. They are the qualities which have proven to be of ultimate importance to the believer and the community of faith in living purposefully, morally, and spiritually.

The predicates do not refer to preexistent hypostatized entities lodged in a mysterious subject and claimed as divine on the grounds that they are so declared by the subject. They are qualities discovered, not invented, tested, lived, and sustained by human beings. These qualities are more suitably described by verbs or adverbs than by noun-substantive locutions. Translating "God is love" or "God has wisdom" or "God possesses compassion" or "God makes peace" into "acting lovingly, or acting wisely, or acting compassionately, or making peace, is godly" emphasizes the significance of human interaction and responsibility. The language stresses the active role of the persons whose believing-behavior testifies to the power of the qualities. Predicate theology takes to heart the biblical anthropology which elevates the human being as divinely imaged. The human figure is not set in opposition to a subject God. He is a figure who has the capacity to experience, express, and cultivate godliness.

Neither humanity nor nature nor history is God. Godliness is discovered within humanity, within nature, and within history by the human subject. The dichotomizing of real and ideal, faith and morality, God and man is fostered by the splitting of subject and predicate. Predicate theology points to the continuities which bind means and ends, fact and value, humanity and divinity. A moral theodicy must satisfy the principle of ideality without falsifying the principle of reality; it must acknowledge the reality of evil without destroying the reality of the moral ideal. A predicate-oriented theology strives to overcome the accusatory character of traditional theodicy, whose subject-predicate bifurcations spawn systems of blame, guilt, and condemnation.

Is Predicate Theology Subjective?

Subject theology has grammar on its side. Bishop Berkeley long ago observed how grammatical convention makes us "apt to think every noun substantive stands for a distinctive idea that may be separated from all others: which hath occasioned infinite mistakes."[23] "God" is such a noun substantive, and it suggests the location of some separate entity. Much in the manner that a noun is separate from its adjectives, a substance is understood as separate from its qualities. The ontological bewitchment of language (Wittgenstein) is nowhere better illustrated than in the conversion of the grammatical subject into a metaphysical substance. No proper grammatical sentence can consist of adjectives alone. Grammatically, therefore, there must be some substantive word which the adjectives modify. Ontologically, it is argued that the qualities need some substantive entity to modify. We recall how John Locke argued that though our ideas are formed of perceived qualities, and though substance is not perceivable, the latter nevertheless must somehow exist. There must be a substratum to support the qualities. Substance cannot be described by its qualities and cannot be perceived, yet substance is "something we know not what." We have noted that many theologians similarly assume that there must be something or someone which exists separate from the attributes. The divine subject is said to be independent of the attributes. What can be said of this attributeless subject? It refers to God-in-Himself, to the absolute being who is who He is. For mystics as well, God-in-Himself can only be named with the help of words which are no real names at all: "the Root of all Roots," "Great Reality," "Indifferent Unity," "*En Sof*, the Limitless."[24] With regard to the subject God's own nature alone, the attitude of the Kabbalah is one of "mystical agnosticism."[25] The positive attributes of the living God of religion do not touch the hem of the skirt of God-in-Himself. He is someone we know not what.

By definition, no unknowable God can be known. Nothing can be said of that which in itself is beyond our comprehension. Whatever is claimed as knowledge of God must therefore be relational. God as revealed to human beings is not God-in-Himself. Predicate theology openly acknowledges an anthropological constant in all our encounters and theological claims. Accordingly, "God" is not a substantive noun which refers to things as they are in themselves, e.g., silver, stone, wood. "God" is a functional noun which can be understood in terms of its relation to others. Mordecai M. Kaplan, the founding philosopher of Reconstructionism, maintains that "God" is properly understood as a functional correlative term. God and person are each related to and dependent upon the other.[26] To speak of God without person is akin to speaking of parents without children or shepherd without sheep or citizen without state or teacher without pupil. Remove the correlative relationship and its meaning dissolves. Clearly the predicates identified and named as divine imply a crucial human component. We have argued that the normal moral connotation of goodness has as its significant referent the human being and humanity, and that events and acts are judged morally in terms of their effect upon them.

The epistemological and axiological centrality of humanity in predicate thinking may open it to the charge that it is a form of subjective idealism and that its values are relative to human needs, desires, and aims. Upon closer examination all theology is inextricably bound to the anthropological predicament, and in that sense is caught up on some level of subjectivity. It is an absurd expectation which would call for the elimination of the subject in order to assure true objectivity.[27] In *The Essence of Christianity,* Feuerbach contended: "If thou doubtest the objective truth of the predicates, thou must also doubt the objective truth of the subject whose predicates they are." To pursue his challenge further we may ask in what sense the idea of the Unmoved Mover or of the divine personality is less relative to human needs and desires than the idea of the sacred predicates. Hartshorne, for example, faults classical theology with a subjectivistic bias. He claims that the "will to power" is a motivating factor in leading its theologians to favor cause over effect and activity over passivity in their characterization of God. He lays "failure of nerve" and a lazy or despairing quest for more security at the feet of the philosophers of classic theology. These emotional and volitional biases, he claims, may account for their preferences for permanence and being over novelty and becoming.[28] The sword opposing subjectivism, however, cuts both ways. How can it exempt Hartshorne's own theological predilections for change, growth, and process from individual and cultural bias? It has been claimed that theologies which herald the process which often contradicts the limited interest of human beings (Hartshorne, Wieman) or those like Barth's, in which a wholly other God stands over against man, are immune to the charge of subjectivism. Yet, the human need for structure and order may call forth a stern and independent

God as anthropocentrically motivated as any subjective *deus pro me*. Masochistic demands may incline toward a punishing deity. The point in all this is that all theological systems are subject to such psychogenetic speculations. The objectivist's charge of subjectivism boomerangs.

Are the Predicates Real?

In our view, the human subject is bound to the world. We favor a phenomenological account of the correlation of man and world, which eliminates the hard disjunctive thinking of either subjectivity or objectivity. The reality of the world is the appearing reality for the human subject. The phenomenon experienced is not and cannot be reality-in-itself but "that which shows itself, the self-revealing, the manifest, in other words, the appearing-being-itself."[29] We experience the "reality-in-itself-for-us." Equally, we experience godliness-in-itself-for-us. The qualities or predicates are not arbitrary inventions of the human spirit, though imagination plays an important part in rehearsing the realm of possibilities. Though their origin may arise from human needs, desires, and wants, the qualities are tested against the stones of reality. The fantasies of human desire are corrigible. An immature experience may be content simply to enjoy its wishful thinking. "But a brief course in experience enforces reflection; it requires but a brief time to teach that some things sweet in the having are bitter in the after-taste and in what they lead to. Primitive innocence does not last."[30]

It is important here to differentiate the reality of experience from the experience of reality. The reality of experience, whether dreamed or not, cannot be questioned. What is questionable is the claimed experience of reality. The latter is tested in terms of its coherence with other claims, the consequences which flow from its affirmation, and its inter-subjective agreement. A vital continuity exists between facts and value. Ideals have roots in natural conditions. While they cannot be reduced to facts, ideals soon discover what nature can sustain and what it finds insupportable. Which ideals are realizable and which are not is an essential part of the process of the discovery of the divine qualities. They are carved out of the tablets of consequences. In what sense, for example, do we speak of "love" as being real? Certainly not in the sense that it is like an object or a person; certainly not in the sense that it is real in and of itself. We speak of love as being real in that it is experienced as "really important" and that it moves us to feel and to act in particular ways. But if we suspect its authenticity, there are ways in which we soon learn to distinguish between love and infatuation, and between one-sided love and reciprocated love. Love bears consequences. Love is not alone something felt but a quality which contains an ideal element to be realized. There is a yearning for love, as for divinity, which is part of its reality.

The transaction of the real and ideal is an active engagement. The ideals are not floating in a preexistent realm to be passively acknowledged. They are potentialities to be actualized, aims to be achieved, ideals that are to be made real. A fascinating rabbinic text illustrates the complementary character of the human and the divine as exemplified in the transaction between the human being and his environment. Akiba, the rabbinic sage, is asked by Tinneius Rufus, the pagan, "Whose works are greater, those of God or those of man?" Akiba replies that the works of man excel, and as evidence places before him sheaves of wheat and dishes of cakes. Akiba regards the latter as greater not because he would denigrate God. For Akiba God and the human being are not contending forces. The sheaves represent the nonhuman givenness -- the product of seed, water, soil, and sun; the cakes represent the transformation of that givenness, the actualization of the potential for the sake of the sustenance of humanity. It is bread and wine, not sheaves and grapes, which are sanctified in praise of the transaction which with human hands brings the natural process to controlled perfection. The ideals are not the final reality already extant in some realm of being. Rabbinic wisdom expresses the faith which calls for transformation. "Everything needs to be acted upon. The lupine must be soaked, the mustard seed sweetened, the wheat ground, and man must be perfected. Everything requires repair."

Where Are the Predicates Lodged?

How can one speak of peace, love, intelligence, compassion, without positing them in some subject? In what do the adjectives, verbs, and adverbs of predicates inhere? Again we are led to review the bias of grammar, which favors substantives over verbs. This syntactical bias, Bertrand Russell maintains, led classic philosophy to the erroneous belief that "every proposition can be regarded as attributing a property to a single thing, rather than expressing a relation between two or more things."[31] Recalling our discussion of "God" as a correlative term, we may ask where fatherhood is located. Is it located in the man or in the child? Where do values reside? Do they rest in the object or in the subject who evaluates? Where do perceived qualities, such as color, exist? Are they quartered in nature or in the mind of the perceiver? The questions presuppose a substantival way of thinking, a fallacy of simple location. We submit that the qualities perceived are functions of two variables, environmental and organic -- the so-called objective factors, e.g., the nature of the surface, the condition of illumination, on one hand, and the visual apparatus on the other. A world without persons endowed with eyesight would retain the potentiality for color but would be colorless. Similarly values are functions of environmental and organic conditions. Human beings have desires, but whether the objects of their desires are desirable depends upon the observable properties of the objects. Values in a world without desiring persons would exist potentially. They are neither "in" the non-tangible objects nor "in" the desiring subjects but are found "between."[32] Hermann Cohen in his *Religion of Reason* explained the principle of divine-human correlation in a manner compatible with predicate theology. He speaks of "the holy spirit" as the mediating concept in the correlation. "If the holy spirit were to be isolated in a person of its own, the correlation would be destroyed. The holy spirit can be neither God alone nor man alone; but neither can it be God and man at the same time; it is an attribute of both, or rather the connection of both."[33]

But can one use terms like "divine," "godly," or "godliness" without referring to a separate, independent Person or Process? Can we speak meaningfully of goodness without locating it in some super-subject? Why not? Do we not use terms like "evil" without reference to Satan? Surely the reality of love and beauty can be understood without reference to Venus or Aphrodite. The tendency to hypostatize qualities is of psychological interest, but theologians and philosophers have long struggled against that reifying prejudice.

To the question "Where is God?" predicate theology points to the divine attributes themselves, e.g., creativity, truth, compassion. Yet even while the attributes are exemplified and acknowledged, the question "Where is God" persists. We are caught in a particular case of Ryle's category mistake. Gilbert Ryle's questioner sought to know where the university was. After being shown the facilities, faculties, student body, alumni, campus grounds, etc., he still wishes to be shown where it is. His request cannot be answered not because there is no university but because he thinks that "university" is an item of the same logical type as "gymnasium" and "library." One cannot exhibit the university in that manner because it "is just the way in which all that he has already seen is organized."[34] Analogously, the term "God" or "godliness" is of a different logical type than that which is expressed by the predicates. "God" or "godliness" refers to the way the predicates are organized and inter-related. "God" or "godliness" is not a subject endowed with a discrete ontological existence. "God" or "godliness" stripped of predicates is a vacuous concept. Ryle's other example may further help us illustrate our point. Here the questioner is shown the elements which contribute to the esprit de corps of a team. He observes the bowling, batting, and wicket-keeping of his first game of cricket, but insists that he be shown the team spirit. "Certainly exhibiting team spirit is not the same thing as bowling or catching, nor is it a third thing such that we can say that the bowler first bowls *and* then exhibits team spirit or that a fielder is at a given moment *either* catching *or* displaying esprit de corps."[35] Accordingly, "God" or "godliness" is not yet another quality which can be added alongside the loving, trusting, caring qualities experienced in our relationships as godly. To do so is to ontologize the logical function of relationship and coordination of godliness and to treat it as if it were a mysterious quality without identifiable characteristics.

Are the Predicates One?

In what sense is "God" or "godliness" one? The unity is not determined by a singular being in which the qualities inhere. The unity is in the shared commonality of the qualities themselves. What do the qualities which are said to manifest godliness have in common? They are united in their loyalty to the superordinate ideal of goodness. The attributes are internally related in their common aim to sustain and advance the quality of living which is characterized as godly. By themselves individual qualities such as wisdom, creativity, and justice are morally ambivalent. Wisdom without compassion sours into manipulative power. Mercy without justice slips into maudlin irresponsibility. In isolation from each other, virtues are blind. Integrated, they exhibit an interdependence which unifies the self and society. Of themselves the qualities are only potentially godly. It is the governing criterion of goodness which qualifies their status as godly. The goodness which the godly qualities serve is experienced as a unification of self and the world. In Dewey's words, "The inclusiveness of the end in relation to both self and the 'universe' to which an inclusive self is related is indispensable"[36] for determining its religious quality.

The stability of the meaning of goodness cannot be assured by fiat. No subject can simply be appealed to in order to fix the meaning for all times and for all people. The believer may appeal to the consequences of sustaining the ideals which are intersubjectively agreed upon. In this sense, "Agreement is the first criterion of truth."[37] In community, the predicates of divinity are consensually validated. Where no such agreement can be obtained, the pluralistic character of belief is upheld. Predicate theology can promise no less frequency of debate than do the varieties of subject theology. The advantage of the former, however, lies in its human comprehensibility, which enables intelligent discourse. One cannot enjoy such examination with claims which are said to originate in the inscrutable will of an Absolute Subject.

Predicate Theodicy: "Why Did It Happen?"

Summing up his ministry the minister confessed that he had spent the first half of his career informing his flock that God is a loving God and that for the remainder of his career he spent his energies explaining why He isn't. In their interpretations of the universe and of the nature of God, theologies raise unreal expectations and foreshadow their theodicies. The mind-set of traditional theology cultivates the expectations of the believer and, with the failure of their realization, conditions him to ask certain kinds of questions and to accept as valid only certain kinds of answers. The believer confronted by a serious illness, for example, may be expected to pray to God who heals. The liturgical form reflects a linear causal relationship between the subject and the patient. Should the patient recover, all praise is due to Him who saves. Should he fail to recover, theological explanation must refer to the subject as well. However the competence of the attending physicians and the strength of the patient may be involved in the outcome, the believer considers them secondary factors. They are regarded as ancillary agents of the primary cause of sickness and health, the singular divine subject. The subject may govern the affairs of the world obliquely, use the auxiliary elements and agents according to His inscrutable design. In the last analysis, behind the screen of natural conditions, it is the Subject of History and Nature who presides, whether by "luring" or by direct intervention or by granting permission.

The very framing of the question, "Why did it happen?" "Why did he have to suffer?", presupposes a number of unarticulated notions which rule out of order certain "obvious" answers. Scientific answers which explain "how" it happened and "what happened" are not satisfactory. They may be appropriate in the realm of impersonal events, e.g., "Why did the metal expand?" but such explanations appear frivolous and demeaning in answer to the question, "Why was my child blinded?" To cite a medical report, to refer to congenital factors or those of contagion or accident, will be grudgingly acknowledged only to be followed by "why" questions of another order. "Why did it happen to *my* child? Why did it happen *now*? Why did it happen *to me*?" The questions are limitless. They seek only those answers which share the tacit assumptions of the question. Such "why" questions demand "who" answers. The "why" questions grow out of a mode of thinking which understands the personal events of the universe as results of the will of personal purposive agents. "Why" means "for what purpose or cause or reason was this done to me and mine?"

To resolve the patent discrepancy between the moral promise on the one hand, and the suffering of the innocents and the prosperity of the unrighteous on the other, the defenders of God exercise their mind-reading of the inscrutable subject. Though His will be unknowable, somehow the theologian knows that it is willed for our good. Though His moral predicates are not ours, somehow the theologian knows that they are good and good for us. Though our afflictions make us weep, somehow they flow from His permission and are thus at bottom good for us, if not now then posthumously. The affliction is real enough, and the real agent cannot be a power other than God. Therefore, the affliction must be deserved. Only the brazen are unable to find some inadequacy in self or in related selves which would justify such chastisement. The very denial of culpability is testimony of their guilt. The believers will eschew hubris and submit to religious masochism. They may find consolation in setting the burden of grief upon the shoulders of the subject. Far better to live safe in His redeeming mystery than to live in the presence of unspeakable atrocities over which persons have no control.

The haunting question "why me?" cannot be answered on its own terms. Entailed in the "why" is an unstated set of presuppositions about the character of the world and of God. It rises out of a theological atmosphere of occult powers exercised upon the world. "Why?" means "what for?" It calls for deciphering the hidden motives of a supramoral and suprapersonal Ego. The manner in which the problem of evil is formulated is unanswerable not because it is intrinsically so complex but because it begs the question. To answer the question according to the demands of the questioner is to submit to the assumptions under dispute. For answers which deny those presuppositions, there is no recourse but to redirect the question.

The tragic character of an event does not imply the presence of a purposive agent lurking behind it. It does not automatically indicate that there is a "who" which directs such occurrences and whose intent it is our theological task to uncover. If events of this order have "meaning" it does not imply that some suprahuman energy deliberately planned their occurrence in order to judge us. Meanings are wrested out of chaos and absurdity. What endows them with sanctity is not their purported origin in the mysterious will of a divine subject, but the character of the interpretation through which we shape constructive response out of destructive event. That a spark of meaning may be salvaged from the darkness does not explain or justify the cause of the catastrophe. Contrary to popular assumption, it is not natural to ask "why" in the sense of "what for" before the presence of every tragedy which befalls humanity. That response to tragedy is theologically conditioned. A predicate-oriented theological view would not give rise to that kind of question, nor would it expect an answer in terms of a supernatural teleology. "Why" need not be construed as soliciting theoretical or empirical information but may be heard as a terrifying cry of distress. "Why" in this instance is equivalent to "woe." To this outcry the proper response is not a scientific or theological explanation but a compassionate arm around the other's shoulders. What is asked for is no analysis of causes, only the presence of a supportive other, an ear which listens without judgment. For those who find consolation in the promise of a world controlled by an unfathomable Agent and of an ultimate reward, nothing can or should be said. For those, however, who feel that such strategies insult their common moral sense and observation, and like Job refuse to accept the presupposition of an accusatory theodicy, another way must be found. For it is not God who fails them but the way that

God has been conceptualized. For them the contradictions between the moral ideal and the reality need not result in apostasy. With reflection and candor, the conflicts may yield different discoveries about the nature of God and the world.

From Whence Ungodliness?

To return to our opening discussion of the prayer for the sick, the inversionary principle interprets differently the disturbing events and the healing process. Sickness, suffering, and death are unequivocally real and evil. Persons may overcome the severity of their blows, may even grow stronger in coping with them. But such courageous responses do not justify their presence. The heroism of the sightless manifests qualities we may rightly call godly; it does not legitimate the loss of sight and make it good. "Woe unto them who say of evil it is good, and of good it is evil; that change darkness into light and light into darkness; that change bitter into sweet and sweet into bitter."[38]

Whence this ungodliness? For subject theology the roots of all events are traced vertically above, originating in the will and wisdom of a hypostatized subject. Its logic personifies good and generates angels and is not less likely to personify evil and generate demons. Fearing the heresy of dualism, all events below are said to originate from one source above, from the One who "forms light and creates darkness, makes peace and creates evil" (Isaiah 45). Such absorption in one governing subject threatens to blur moral distinctions.

In predicate thinking, the vertical line is bent horizontal. Evils are real and are of many sorts. The predicates of evil are experienced as real, as are the predicates of good. Neither set of predicates requires a subject, divine or demonic, to explain their origin and power. Evils are not the work of a malevolent suprapersonal will, but acts and events which threaten human growth, equilibrium, and fulfillment. Their causes may be unknown, but their mystery is not due to their origin in some occult satanic agency. They are not sent down or up from a demonic realm designed to hurt or punish innocence. Evils are of all kinds and are all subject to analysis and investigation, social, economic, political, psychological, medical. However awful their consequences, they originate from the natural soil in which we live and must be coped with accordingly. Allowed to be mystified, radicalized, and reified, evils are transmuted into a suprapersonal demonic threat before which human beings can do nothing but wring their hands or wait upon a suprapersonal benevolent force to counter the enemy. Understood as natural aberrations of natural forces, the variety of their forms may be dealt with, some actively resisted, some accepted, some sublimated, each according to its own nature.

A powerfully suggestive myth on the nature and forms of evil is recorded in the Talmud, which tells of the capture of the Evil Tempter. The captors sought to kill it but were warned that with its destruction, the entire world would fall apart. They imprisoned it nonetheless. Three days later they looked throughout the land for a fresh egg and could not find one, for when the sexual drive is extirpated, no eggs are available; where the libido is destroyed, civilization is ended. Those who held the Evil Tempter captive were themselves held fast in the vise of a dilemma. If they killed the Tempter, the world would be unable to endure; if they let it loose, evil would be free to roam the land. The captors begged for half-mercy, asking that the Tempter should live but not tempt. To this request the divine echo responded, "They do not grant halves in heaven."[39] The myth reminds man that evil is often mixed with good, and that some forms of evil possess energies which when properly sublimated can serve for good. Without justifying evil, the myth speaks to the ambivalence and naturalness of evil as well as to the ways it can and cannot be confronted.

Natural Evil

What then is the relationship between nature and divinity, and what do we make of the havoc that nature sometimes creates? God or godliness is discovered within nature by the light of the selective principle which searches for powers and energies to uplift man. Following predicate theology, the appropriate religious stance toward nature is one of natural piety. "Is it not our own substance? Are we made of other clay? All our possibilities lie from eternity hidden in its bosom . . . we may address it without superstitious terrors; it is not wicked. It follows its own habits abstractedly."[40] No deification or demonization is called for. Nature is neutral, potential, and amoral. Godliness is discovered within nature as the indispensable source for our life and in our transformation of its possibilities for human joy. Divinity is not in the acts of nature but in the human control of its floods and destruction. Lightning, earthquake, and tempest are no "acts of God," a definition which lawyers use (*Bouvier's Law Dictionary*) and doctors of theology feel compelled to conjure with. The purported "acts of God" are catastrophes which theodicies construe as hiding God's silver lining. From our perspective, there is no need for theology to compete with science in offering better or deeper explanations for the tornado and the drought. Religion is not a better explanation or justification. It offers a different appreciation of the amoral powers in nature and the goals toward which nature may be controlled. To the village swept away by the flood, a predicate theology will express its profoundest sympathy, help organize relief, and urge the reclamation of the land. In the acts of encouragement, compassion, mutual aid, and cooperative effort, godliness is expressed. It will not pretend that what nature wrought is God's will. Some of the sages articulated a view of natural evil which is compatible with a predicate perspective. It would be right, the sages declare, for stolen seeds not to sprout and for women raped not to give birth, but "the world pursues its natural course, and stolen seeds sprout as luxuriantly as seeds naturally acquired."[41] The ways of nature are not the ways of God, else it would be nature that should be imitated and not the moral attributes of divinity.

History and Evil

God is not history any more than God is nature. Panhistoricism, which equates God and history, is no less misleading than pantheism, which would identify God and nature. But as with nature, divinity may be discovered within history. History is the arena in which moral ideals emerge, are tested, fail, and succeed. The perversities of the human spirit have multiple causes, which we label as greed, jealousy, sadism, scapegoating, and which stem from many conditions. The roots are complex, but if religious men and women truly mean to prevent their recurrence, if the deeply felt cry "never again" is to be acted upon, theology would do well to abandon the strained justification of God's will along with the invocation of demonic forces as an explanation and exculpation of the Holocaust. It need not conjure up the good or evil intentions of God or Satan but should examine the conditions which unleashed such unspeakable godlessness upon the world. At the same time, it must not lose sight of the acts of human heroism borne witness by the self-sacrifice of tens of thousands who risked their lives and those of their close ones to rescue and protect the hunted. It must raise to high consciousness the acts of cooperation and love which took place in the hellholes of concentration camps and crematoria. For these energies which fed the hungry, healed the sick, loosened the fetters of the bound, upheld the fallen, bound the bruises of the beaten, are precisely the acts of divinity which must be known, blessed, and lived. They constitute the flesh-and-blood testimonies of the reality of godliness. For godliness is not demonstrated logically, it is acted out and testified to existentially. Godliness is better expressed in relational verbs than in isolated nouns because it is in relationship that godliness is realized. The key preposition in predicate theology is not "in" or "beyond" but "with."

The liturgical formulation of the prayer for or by the sick with which we opened our discussion reflects a subject theology. The same prayer in the mode of predicate theology similarly articulates praise and petition of divinity. It is, however, not directed to a subject who, as it were, holds the cure in His hand and must be moved to dispense it to the sick. Prayer is not magic. It is no surrogate for work. Predicate prayer is reflexive in the sense that nothing can be asked another without calling upon the labor of one's own energies. Prayer is not only "poetry believed in" (Santayana), it is poetry acted upon. One cannot praise God with arms folded. From a predicate view, to praise God for making peace or feeding the poor or clothing the naked does not refer to a supernal Other. It refers to the capacities of persons in society to transcend their provincial interests of self and find their realization in the larger Self. No blessings prevail except through the work of human hands. Prayer is multi-functional. But as far as its petitionary role is concerned, it is, for predicate theology, something said in order that something be done by those who say it. Godliness is to be behaved. Subject liturgy is less inclined to direct the worshipper toward such a behavioral posture. It is for this reason that many have found the subject liturgy of praise and petition to cultivate dependence and passivity in the worshipper.

"That which heals the sick" calls the worshipper to set his mind and heart upon the complexity of elements which converge upon the healing process. It calls to mind the "givenness" of nature, the matrix out of which medicines are extracted, along with the activities of researchers, medical practitioners, nurses, family and friends, the inner curative forces of the patient, including trust and courage and self-respect, which restore health. That which in subject theology is taken for granted or dismissed as merely human or natural is sanctified as a manifestation of divinity.

For some, such an unfoldment of the elements which make for recovery is too prosaic. But this is one of the major tasks of predicate theology: to recognize the sanctity of the ordinary, the divinity of the diurnal; to overcome the hard disjunctives which force upon us false either/or alternatives: either the acts of God or the acts of persons, either divinity or humanity, either fact or value.

And where there is no recovery from sickness, where there is instead dying and death, a mature theology will have created a religious atmosphere in which either blaming or excusing a subject is out of the order of expectation and in which self-accusation for purported transgressions is not in place. "Why me?" does not lose its pathos. It does lose its persecutory and accusatory insinuation. It does not deny the genuineness of guilt and the need to make reparation. It does deny that the sickness or death is either the punishment or the reward of a supranatural subject. It does not deny the proper place for repentance and restitution and responsibility. It does deny the notion that whatever misfortune befalls me or mine was caused by sins which brought forth the severe sentence from on high.

It may be reasonably asked whether predicate theology can be emotionally satisfying; whether people can find security in godly qualities in the same manner that they find it in a personified, individualistic subject; whether predicate theodicy can provide the comfort and consolation which comes from belief in a God who gives and takes away. These are important questions to be considered, though they refer more to the psychological efficacy of our theological position than to its intellectual or moral adequacy. But the questions call for some general response. It occurs to us that theological analysis cannot rightly be expected to do the work of ritual or liturgical choreography. This holds for any theology. The theological reflections of a Maimonides or an Aquinas, a Hartshorne or a Wieman, have a different function than that of prayer. Religious expressivity calls upon metaphors and symbols, myths and hymns. Its intention is to move the spiritual imagination of men and women. Even so, faith is more than poetry. It is a way of thinking as well as a way of feeling. Faith must be believed in and acted on and felt to be morally sound. In our times the God-language of subject theology no longer resonates in the depths of the human spirit. We have argued that the fault lies not in the symbols but in what they point to. Like any given theology, predicate theology requires liturgical translation in an appropriate key. There is nothing intrinsic in its formulation to keep the worshipper from passionate commitment and utterance. For many there is comfort in not knowing and consolation in mystification. But there are others for whom the Subject God who governs and decrees life and death produces an atmosphere of blame and guilt. For these the answers given to Job raise more anger and doubt than they hoped to resolve. They find more comfort in understanding the limits of nature, the reality of accident and the human tasks of responsibility and comfort.

Why the Use of God-Terms?

Given the centrality of the notion of goodness in predicate theology, what more is achieved in recasting the moral materials into the locution of godliness? Three considerations commend our usage. First, the identification and naming of the qualities that express the sanctities of our faith commitment raises them out of the dust of ordinariness to the heights of religious consciousness. The activities and events which a bifurcated view devalues as "merely" human are assigned their proper spiritual status. The incorporation of such discovered values into the liturgical vocabulary of our faith-language directs awareness to the tasks and goals to be pursued. God-terms are meant to elevate those vital qualities and events which are characteristically relegated to the prosaic, secular sphere.

Second, the predicates of divinity express the crucial nexus between the faith of our ancestors and our own. However differently the idea of God may be formulated, it is in its attributes that the commonality of our interests and values is articulated. The moral predicates which are to be emulated in our lives unite the generations. Therein lies the *kerygma*, the essential message, of religious faith. Predicate theology maintains that theodicies which house divinity in subject-substantive forms often prevent us from seeing the full moral implications of monotheistic faith for human beings. In demythologizing the ontologizing grammar of subject theology, the divinity of the attributes which surround us and of which we are an active part is revealed. By way of analogy, the myths of the Bible, e.g., the Garden of Eden, the deluge and Tower of Babel, the miracles of the Exodus, remain significant for orthodox and non-orthodox believers not because of their literal meaning for them both but because of the common moral intention which lies at their core. The diverse theological forms in which the predicates are posited ought not to eclipse the sanctity of the predicates.

Third, to establish a monopoly on the use of God-terms for subject theology alone is to arbitrarily arrest theological progress. The briefest rehearsal of the history of each faith's theologies offers indisputable evidence of the variety of interpretations that have been given to the idea of God. To submit to a monolithic semantics would stymie the needed theological response to the moral and intellectual challenges of our time.

The emphasis upon the moral connotation of goodness and the morality of God may lead the reader to the erroneous conclusion that the predicates of divinity and of religious value are exclusively moral. It is true that in our analysis and critique of theodicy we have paid singular attention to the moral consequences of the defense of God. But religion includes an entire gamut of cognitive, affective, aesthetic, and celebratory values which are vital to its life. They have their significant place among the predicates of divinity. While ethical concern and behavior lie at the heart of a moral predicate theology, it means in no way to disregard the amoral and nonmoral values of religion. Myth, ritual, the binding of the community of faith, the mystic and liturgical life are crucial for religion and are interwoven with the fabric of the moral life.

The Loaded Options of Religion's Critics

It is important to note how much of the modern and contemporary criticism of religion is directed toward the God which theodicy presents. It is less the intellectual claims and far more the moral claims for God's existence that receive the attention of such modern critics of religion as Marx, Feuerbach, Freud, Nietzsche, and Sartre. Their antagonism is toward the systems of apology which defend God by accusing humanity: by robbing human beings of their dignity and competence; by rendering them guilty and helpless, and counseling them to sacrifice their moral and activistic competencies; by falsifying the meaning of the terrors of nature and history and urging flight into the sanctuary of ignorance; by raising expectations which run counter to common experience. It is in their conclusions, not in their protestations against traditional theodicies, that we sense their error. For the critics have simply taken the opposite side of the coin and defended man by accusing God. In their substitution of humanity for divinity, they remain blind to the transcendent character of the human being and his discoveries, to the reality of man's genuine sense of dependence, which need not spell his self-denigration, to the dangers in the conceit of men and the idolatries of his self. The critics have correctly been wary of the use of "transcendence," to guarantee the absoluteness and immutability of their values. How indeed are we to guard against those who drape their human opinions in the garments of "His transcendent realm"? Faith healers commonly deny that cures come from their human powers and insist that credit be given to a transcendent source. In this manner their own urgings for control are modestly projected outward only to return to them like a boomerang bathed in the powers of transcendence. But the critics do not distinguish between what we may call vertical and horizontal transcendence. Some of the dangers of the former we have already acknowledged. The latter, however, refers to the transcendence of normatives, to the realm of ideas which express our spiritual yearnings and move us toward their actualization. Such horizontal transcendence is not grounded in a supramoral Absolute Being but in the matrix of selves and community. Transcendence of this order serves as a reminder of the limitations of the status quo. It is essential to the understanding of predicate theology. The radical opposition of transcendence and immanence by the critics of religion is part and parcel of their either/or thinking. They force false options upon us. Thus Feuerbach, in his zeal to overcome the alienation of man from God, identifies the divine and human predicates. The options he presents are simply the other side of either/or subject theology. Either the denigration of man or his apotheosis; divinity is lodged either in the objectivity of the subject or in the subjectivity of man; either the opposition of God and man or their identification. Either the Lord of History and of Nature, the God who justifies the status quo, the God who causes or permits the Holocaust, or else no God but man. They are loaded choices. Predicate theology offers another alternative.

Camus has written that spiritual rebellion can only exist "in a society where theoretical equality conceals great factual inequalities."[42] Theodicies generally appear as concealments of both the pledge of the moral covenant and the factual inequalities which exhibit the terrorizing of the innocent and the flourishing of the guilty. The Jobian rebel denies neither the breach of the covenant nor its sacred promise. His religious fidelity lies in his allegiance to the truth and the good. The answer out of the whirlwind may awe him into momentary silence. It will not last. For the nexus between Yahweh and Job does not lie in a power relationship but in a moral kinship. Job knows and worships that justice and morality which enable him to defend his ways against the sycophantic friends of God. Job will open his mouth again, for he knows that the moral attributes of Yahweh are his advocates even against Yahweh Himself.[43]

Elie Wiesel is a traditionalist, but like many believers, he cannot endure theology as usual after Auschwitz. In his novel *The Accident*, he portrays the tormented spirit of Sarah, the prostitute, victim of the death camps. His hero has heard the story of her tortures and the terrible price she pays for her survival. Enraged, he cries out, "Whoever listens to Sarah and doesn't change, whoever enters Sarah's world and does not invent new gods and new religions, deserves death and destruction." This is not the voice of atheism. It is the sound of those who recognize that theological sameness is no compliment to authentic religious tradition. It is the sound which echoes the religious audacity of tradition and that calls for new ways to understand divinity. The proposal for predicate theology and predicate liturgy, despite the analytic character of its presentation, is offered in response to Wiesel's passionate challenge. It is not meant for everyone. It is for those who are embarrassed by the theological rationalizations which leave God morally defenseless or indifferent to suffering. Predicate theology and theodicy are for those who cannot go home again using old routes, but who choose not to remain homeless.

Notes

Introduction

1. Carl Jung, "Psychology and Religion," in *Collected Works*, vol. II (Princeton University Press, Princeton, N.J., 1958.

2. E. L. Mascall, *The Secularization of Christianity* (New York: Holt, Rienhart & Winston, 1965), p. 44. Mascall oversimplifies the crisis of contemporary unbelief by contending that "the main cause is the continual impact upon the senses of a technocratic culture in which all emphasis falls upon what man can do with things and hardly any upon what they really are."

Michael Novak, *Belief and Unbelief* (New York: Macmillan, 1965), p. 175, assumes that "the most common argument against belief today . . . is not the belief that God is impossible because of theoretical difficulties; the theoretical difficulties appear merely to furnish an excuse." Thus Novak enumerates such external factors as the bad behavior of bishops in princely palaces, the use of obsolete religious metaphors, authoritarianism, and the church's succumbing to middle-class values among the real irritants causing unbelief in our times.

Harvey Cox, *The Secular City* (New York: Macmillan, 1965), p. 63, explains and appears to favor the technopolitan man "who wastes little time thinking about 'ultimate' and 'religious' questions" and who does not agonize over alienation, sickness, and death.

3. Contemporaries such as M. B. Foster, Claude Tresmontant, Friedrich Gogarten, E. L. Mascall, Harvey Cox, Langdon Gilkey, and A. N. Whitehead have credited the biblical idea of creation and the voluntaristic character of the living God with providing the indispensable presuppositions of scientific experimentation. The rigidity of the intelligible forms of Greek theory is said to have been loosened by the biblical idea of an active and free deity whose created world is filled with real contingency. Such a theological view is credited with encouraging an empirical openness to the universe. The de-divinization of the sensible world accomplished through the affirmation of *creatio ex nihilo* is celebrated by the theologians as sanction for scientific experimentation with nature.

Langdon Gilkey, *Maker of Heaven and Earth* (Garden City, N.Y.: Doubleday Anchor Books, 1965), cites the Christian emphasis upon the finiteness and sinfulness of human reason as a factor encouraging the empirical study of the contingent, as opposed to the rational conceit which claims knowledge of the necessary forms. At the same time he calls upon the "image of God" in man as a basic element bolstering man's confidence in his capacity to know the world.

Claude Tresmontant, in "Biblical Metaphysics," *Cross Currents* (n.d.), p. 236, argues that "astronomy as a science would not be possible as long as the stars were considered as divine substances."

See also Harvey Cox, who credits biblical writing with the "disenchantment of nature," "deconsecration of values," and "desacralization of politics" (*Secular City*, chap. I, "The Biblical Sources of Secularization").

4. Martin E. Marty, *Varieties of Unbelief* (New York: Holt, Rinehart & Winston, 1964), p. 57.

5. Brand Blanshard, *Reason and Belief* (London: George Allen & Unwin, 1974), p. 546.

6. Martin Buber, *Between Man and Man* (London: Routledge & Kegan Paul, 1947), p. 132.

7. Hans Jonas, *The Gnostic Religion* (Boston: Beacon Press, 1963), p. 325. "If not science and technology, what caused, for the human groups involved, the collapse of the cosmic piety of classical civilization, on which so much of its ethics was built?" (p. 330).

8. Ibid., p. 330.

9. Max Weber, *The Sociology of Religion* (Boston: Beacon Press, 1963).

10. Paul Tillich, *Systematic Theology*, vol. III (Chicago: University of Chicago Press, 1963), p. 404.

11. Martin Buber, *The Prophetic Faith* (New York: Harper Torchbooks, 1960), p. 183.

12. Stephen Toulmin, *Reason in Ethics* (New York: Cambridge University Press, 1964), p. 213.

13. C. L. Stevenson, *Ethics and Language* (New Haven: Yale University Press, 1944).

14. Arthur O. Lovejoy, *The Great Chain of Being* (New York: Harper & Brothers, 1960), pp. 5, 6.

15. H. R. Niebuhr, *Radical Monotheism and Western Culture* (New York: Harper & Brothers, 1960), p. 32.

Chapter I

1. George Santayana, *Reason in Religion* (New York: Collier Books, 1962), p. 133.

2. Gabriel Marcel, *The Mystery of Being* (New York: Gateway Editions, 1960).

3. William James, *The Varieties of Religious Experience* (New York: Longmans, Green, 1929.

4. Pascal, *Pensées* (New York: Random House, 1941), frag. 205.

5. Franz Kafka, *Parables* (New York: Schocken Books, 1947).

6. Moses Maimonides, *Guide of the Perplexed* I:53.

7. Paul Tillich identified the religious character of this intellectual passion. See his chapter on "Reason and Revelation" in *Systematic Theology* (Chicago: University of Chicago Press, 1963), vol. 1; also Michael Polanyi's evaluation of the commitment of "personal knowledge." The religious character of knowledge is apparent in the Platonic conception of philosophy as a "turning of the soul from becoming into being" (*Republic* 518c); and in Aristotle's acknowledgment of reason as divine. We are to "make ourselves immortal, and strain every nerve to live in accordance with the best in us" (*Nichomachean Ethics* 1178a).

8. See John Cobb's *A Christian Natural Theology* (Philadelphia: Westmin-

ster Press, 1965), in which an intellectual approach to God, along Whiteheadian lines, is regarded as essential to his spiritual existence as a Christian (p. 14).

From the time of Clement of Alexandria, the notion was held that the intellect was the sole element in human nature with the capacity to get into true contact with the divine nature. See R. H. Flew, *The Idea of Perfection in Christian Theology* (New York: Oxford University Press, 1934).

9. Maimonides, *Guide of the Perplexed* III:51.

10. Ibid., III:17.

11. Ibid., III:22.

12. Ibid., III:12.

13. Ibid., I:53.

14. Ibid., I:50; see also III:51.

15. St. Thomas Aquinas, *Summa Theologica* I, Q. 12, a. 1.

16. Ibid., I, Q. 22, a. 1; art. 2 refers to "Rabbi Moses" (Maimonides) who excluded men from the order of corruptible things because of their intellectual excellence.

17. Pascal, *Pensées*, frag. 347.

18. Job 42:1-6.

19. Benedict Spinoza, *Ethics*, pt. IV, note to prop. XVIII.

20. Michael Novak, *Belief and Unbelief* (New York: Macmillan, 1965), p. 125.

21. Aristotle, *Eudemian Ethics* VII, 1244b. For Aristotle, as for Spinoza, to ascribe love to God demeans Him, subjecting Him to man's changing passions, sufferings, and aspirations. "God does not love or hate anyone," Spinoza argues in his *Ethics*, pt. IV, prop. XVIII.

22. Aristotle, *Metaphysics*, bk. XII, chap. 9 (30).

23. Maimonides, *Guide of the Perplexed*, I:58.

24. Judah Halevi, *Kitab al Khuzari* (New York: Schocken Books, 1964), pp. 200 and 218.

25. Ibid.

26. Martin Buber, "Religion and Philosophy," in *The Eclipse of God* (New York: Harper & Brothers, 1952), p. 32.

27. Paul Tillich, *Theology of Culture*, ed. Robert Kimball (New York: Oxford University Press, 1964), p. 10. The author is characterizing what he refers to as the "ontological type of philosophy of religion."

28. Martin Buber, *I and Thou* (New York: Charles Scribner's Sons, 1958), p. 100.

29. Karl Barth, *Church Dogmatics* (Edinburgh: T. & T. Clark, 1961), vol. IV, pt. 3, p. 457. In *The Doctrine of the Word of God* (New York: Charles Scribner's Sons, 1936), p. 234, Barth speaks of acknowledgment of the word of God as related to "the presence of a definite power of disposal, positive or negative, respecting the person who acknowledges something. But acknowledgment means not only submission to a necessity, but self-adaptation to the stark objectivity of the necessity, acceptance of it as good, not merely

finding oneself in it, but seeing one's way about it."

30. Emil Brunner, *The Divine-Human Encounter* (Philadelphia: Westminster Press, 1943), p. 74.

31. From an unpublished manuscript on "Theological Analysis" by Charles McCoy. (Pacific School of Religion, Berkeley, California, 1968).

32. Aquinas, *Summa Theologica* I, Q. 6, a. 1.

33. Ibid.

34. Ludwig Feuerbach, *The Essence of Christianity* (New York: Harper & Brothers, 1957).

Chapter 2

1. Stephen Toulmin, *Foresight and Understanding* (New York: Harper & Row, 1961), p. 57.

2. Ibid., p. 44.

3. Ibid., p. 42.

4. E. L. Mascall, *Existence and Analogy* (Archon Books: Hamden, Connecticut, 1969), p. 66.

5. Martin Buber, "Samuel and Agag," in *The Philosophy of Martin Buber* (LaSalle, Ill.: Open Court, 1967).

6. Ibid., p. 32.

7. John Stuart Mill, *An Examination of Sir William Hamilton's Philosophy* (London: Library of Little Arts, 1867), pp. 119-129.

8. Aristotle, *Nichomachean Ethics* X, 1178 (10).

9. Ibid., 1178 (20).

10. St. Anselm, *Proslogion* (LaSalle, Ill.: Open Court, 1903), chaps. 1-4.

11. Harry A. Wolfson, *The Philosophy of Spinoza* (New York: Schocken Books, 1969), pp. 167f., vol. 1.

12. Moses Maimonides, *Guide of the Perplexed*, III:19.

13. Toulmin, *Foresight and Understanding*, p. 101. In *The Structure of Scientific Revolutions* (University of Chicago Press: Chicago, 1962), p. 108, T. S. Kuhn has argued that scientific schools which disagree about what is the problem and what is the solution "inevitably talk through each other when debating the relative merits of their respective paradigms. In the partially circular arguments that regularly result, each paradigm will be shown to satisfy more or less the criteria it dictates for itself and to fall short of a few of those dictated by its opponent."

14. Ludwig Wittgenstein, *Philosophical Investigations*, trans. G. E. M. Anscombe (New York: Oxford University Press, 1953), p. 113.

15. Michael Polanyi, *Personal Knowledge* (New York: Harper & Row, 1962), p. 267.

16. Charles McCoy, "Theological Analysis," unpublished manuscript.

17. Herbert Feigl, in an article "De Principus non Disputandum," privately circulated, draws such a distinction between justification and vindication. A later formulation of his argument may be found in his contribution

to *Philosophical Analysis*, ed. Max Black (Ithaca, N.Y.: Cornell University Press, 1950).

18. St. Thomas Aquinas, *Summa Theologica*, I, Q. 2, a. 3.

19. Ibid.

20. Ibid.

21. Ibid., I, Q. 2, a. 1.

22. Ibid., I, Q2, a. 3.

23. Ibid., emphasis added.

24. St. Thomas Aquinas, *Summa Contra Gentiles* I, chap. 11.

25. *Summa Theologica* I, Q. 13, a. 2.

26. Ibid., I, Q. 13, a. 3.

Chapter 3

1. St. Thomas Aquinas, *Summa Contra Gentiles* I, chap. 74.

2. St. Thomas Aquinas, *Summa Theologica* I, Q. 19, a. 1.

3. Ludwig Feuerbach, *The Essence of Christianity* (New York: Harper & Brothers, 1957), pp. 37ff.

4. Aquinas, *Summa Theologica* I, Q. 14, a. 10.

5. Aristotle, *Metaphysics*, bk. XII, 1075a.

6. Aquinas, *Summa Theologica* I, Q. 14, a. 1.

7. Maimonides, *Guide of the Perplexed* I:52.

8. Ibid.

9. Charles Hartshorne, *Man's Vision of God* (Chicago: Willet, Clark & Co., 1941), pp. 98ff.

10. Maimonides, *Guide of the Perplexed*, III:54.

11. Ibid., I:54.

12. Aquinas, *Summa Theologica* I, Q. 4, a. 8.

13. R. N. Flew, *The Idea of Perfection in Christian Theology* (London: Oxford University Press, 1934).

14. Aquinas, *Summa Theologica* I, Q. aa, a. 1, 2.

15. B. J. Lonergan, *Insight: A Study of Human Understanding* (London: Longman's, Green & Co., 1958), pp. 249-254, 291ff.

16. Aquinas, *Summa Theologica*, F, Q. 48, a. 1.

17. St. Augustine, *Enchiridion* IV:13, in *Confessions and Enchiridion* (Philadelphia: Westminster Press, 1955).

18. Aquinas, *Summa Theologica*, I, Q. 49, a. 1.

19. Aquinas, *Summa Contra Gentiles*, chap. 20; cf. *Summa Theologica*, I, Q. 47, a. 1.

20. Aquinas, *Summa Theologica* I, Q. 48, a. 2.

21. Ibid., I, Q. 48, a. 2: "Non est omnia, si essent aequalia."

22. Aquinas, *Summa Contra Gentiles*, chap. 71; cf. *Summa Theologica*, I, Q. 48, a. 2.

23. G. W. Leibniz, *Theodicy*, pt. II, par. 121; cf. Aquinas, *Summa Contra Gentiles*, chap. 71.

24. *Summa Contra Gentiles* III, chap. 71.

25. Leibniz, *Theodicy*, II, par. 118.

26. Aquinas, *Summa Theologica* I, Q. 95, a. 1; cf. *Summa Contra Gentiles*, chap. 7.

27. Spinoza, *Ethics*, II, definition VI: "Reality and Perfection, I use as synonymous terms." In letter 32 to Blyenberg, Spinoza refers to Adam's eating the forbidden fruit not as an evil act but as one which "includes perfection insofar as it expresses reality."

28. Plato, *Laws* X, 903a.

29. Maimonides, *Guide of the Perplexed* III:22.

30. Ibid., III:12.

31. Leibniz, *Theodicy*, pt. II, par. 118.

32. Ibid., pt. I, par. 19.

33. Ibid., pt. II, par. 124.

34. Ibid., pt. II, par. 118.

35. Karl Barth, *Church Dogmatics* (Edinburgh: T. & T. Clark, 1961), vol. III, pt. 3, sec. 50, p. 318.

36. Ibid., p. 317.

37. Aquinas, *Summa Contra Gentiles*, chap. 71.

38. Ibid.

39. Aquinas, *Summa Theologica* I, chap. 48, Q. 25, a. 6.

40. Leibniz, *Theodicy*, pt. II, par. 117.

41. Aquinas, *Summa Theologica* I, Q. 25, a. 6.

Chapter 4

1. The term "quasi-theism" is used by Edward Madden and Peter Hare in their *Evil and the Concept of God* (Springfield, Ill.: Charles C. Thomas, 1968). It refers to theologies which seek to combine the best features of a theistic God "with the desirable ones of a temporal or pantheistic God" (p. 104).

2. Charles Hartshorne, *Man's Vision of God* (Chicago: Willet, Clark & Co., 1941), p. 93.

3. Charles Hartshorne, *The Logic of Perfection* (LaSalle, Ill.: Open Court, 1962), p. 142.

4. Charles Hartshorne and William Reese, *Philosophers Speak of God* (Chicago: University of Chicago Press, 1953), p. 110.

5. Hartshorne, *Logic of Perfection*, p. 314.

6. Ibid., p. 314.

7. Ibid., p. 309.

8. Hartshorne, *Man's Vision of God*, p. 203.

9. Hartshorne and Reese, *Philosophers Speak of God*, p. 110.

10. Hartshorne, *Man's Vision of God*, p. 157.

11. Hartshorne, *Logic of Perfection*, p. 310.

12. Ibid., p. 314, cf. p. 309.

13. Alfred North Whitehead, *Adventures of Ideas* (New York: Macmillan,

1933), p. 345.

14. Ibid., pp. 341-342.

15. Ibid., p. 336.

16. Ibid., p. 331.

17. Alfred North Whitehead, *Process and Reality* (New York: Harper & Row, 1960), p. 531.

18. Stephen Lee Ely, *The Religious Availability of Whitehead's God* (Wisconsin: University of Wisconsin Press, 1942), p. 41.

19. David Ray Griffin, *God, Power and Evil* (Philadelphia: Westminster Press, 1976), pp. 301-302.

20. Henry Nelson Wieman, *The Source of Human Good* (Carbondale: Southern Illinois University Press, 1946), p. 79.

21. Ibid., p. 79.

22. Ibid., p. 81.

23. Ibid.

24. Ibid., p. 80.

25. Ibid., p. 116.

26. Henry Nelson Wieman, *The Directive in History* (Boston: Beacon Press, 1949), p. 47.

27. John B. Cobb, Jr., *Living Options in Protestant Theology* (Philadelphia: Westminster Press, 1962), p. 113.

28. Wieman, *Source of Human Good*, p. 223.

29. Wieman, *Directive in History*, p. 30.

30. Ibid., p. 43.

31. Ibid., p. 123.

32. Robert Bretall, ed., *The Empirical Theology of Henry Nelson Wieman* (New York: Macmillan, 1963), p. 287.

33. Wieman, *Source of Human Good*, pp. 55, 73, 75, 76, 81, et passim.

34. Wieman, *Directive in History*, p. 50.

35. Ibid., p. 74.

36. Ibid., p. 69.

37. Wieman, *Source of Human Good*, p. 117.

38. Ibid.

39. Ibid., p. 92.

40. Ibid., p. 224.

41. Ibid., pp. 89-90.

42. Paul Tillich, *Systematic Theology* (Chicago: University of Chicago Press, 1963), vol. I, p. 244.

43. F. W. J. Schelling, *Of Human Freedom* (LaSalle, Ill.: Open Court, 1936), p. 80.

44. Ibid., p. 95.

45. Tillich, *Systematic Theology*, vol. I, pp. 246-247.

46. Ibid., p. 269.

47. Ibid., p. 270.

48. Ibid., p. 245.

49. B. Talmud, *Avodah Zarah* 54b.

50. Tillich, *Systematic Theology*, vol. I, p. 156.

51. Paul Tillich, *Biblical Religion and the Search for Ultimate Reality* (Chicago: University of Chicago Press, 1955), p. 84.

52. Tillich, *Systematic Theology*, vol. I, pp. 266-267.

53. Psalm, 72:12f.

54. Paul Tillich, *The Courage to Be* (New Haven: Yale University Press, 1959), p. 181.

55. Tillich, *Systematic Theology*, vol. I, p. 244.

56. Tillich, *Biblical Religion*, p. 75.

57. Tillich, *Systematic Theology*, vol. I, p. 280.

58. Ibid., p. 284.

59. Ludwig Feuerbach, *The Essence of Christianity* (New York: Harper & Brothers, 1957), app. 11, p. 300.

60. Tillich, *Systematic Theology*, vol. I, p. 271.

61. Tillich, *Biblical Religion*, p. 81.

62. Ibid.

63. Tillich, *Systematic Theology*, vol. I, p. 272.

64. Ibid., p. 271.

65. Abraham H. Maslow, *Toward a Psychology of Being* (New York: Van Nostrand, 1962), p. 70.

66. Ibid., p. 72.

67. Ibid., p. 88.

68. Ibid., p. 79.

69. Ibid., p. 86.

Chapter 5

1. St. Thomas Aquinas, *Summa Theologica*, I, Q. 13, a. 7.

2. John L. McKenzie, *The Two-Edged Sword* (New York: Image Books, 1966), chap. XVI.

3. *Psalms* 44:21.

4. Henry Aiken, *Reason and Conduct* (New York: Alfred A. Knopf, 1962), p. 182.

5. Ludwig Koehler, *Old Testament Theology* (London: Lutterworth Press, 1957), p. 62.

6. Genesis 18:19.

7. Amos 3:7.

8. Jeremiah 22:15; cf. 5:28, 7:5f., 9:23.

9. Genesis 18:25.

10. J. B. Soloveitchik, "The Lonely Man of Faith," *Tradition*, Summer 1965.

11. Psalms 44:18ff.

12. Koehler, *Old Testament Theology*, pp. 24f.

13. Exodus 33:23.

14. Isaiah 45:7.

15. Talmud, *Sanhedrin* 96b.

16. *Amos* 3:6.

17. Karl Barth, *Church Dogmatics*, (Edinburgh: T. & T. Clark, 1961), vol. IV, pt. 3, sec. 70.

18. Job 16:19-21.

19. Barth, *Church Dogmatics*, p. 428.

20. Ibid.

21. Ibid., p. 431.

22. Ibid., p. 405.

23. Ibid., p. 407.

24. Ibid., p. 457.

25. Ibid., p. 460.

26. Ibid., vol. II, pt. 1, p. 300.

27. Ibid., p. 284.

28. Ibid., p. 296.

29. Ibid., p. 496.

30. Ibid., p. 324.

31. Ibid., p. 171.

32. Helmut Gollwitzer, *The Existence of God as Confessed by Faith* (Philadelphia: Westminster Press, 1965), pp. 103f.

33. Barth, *Church Dogmatics*, vol. II, pt. 2, p. 334.

34. John Hick, *Evil and the God of Love* (New York: Harper & Row, 1966), p. 41.

35. Barth, *Church Dogmatics*, vol. III, pt. 3, p. 35.

36. In his *The Sacred Canopy* (New York: Doubleday Anchor Books, 1969), Peter Berger employs this term in a non-Freudian sense. It refers to the self-denying surrender of the individual to large nomoi (pp. 55f.).

37. Herbert W. Richardson, *Toward an American Theology* (New York: Harper & Row, 1967), p. 10.

38. Walter Eichrodt, *Theology of the Old Testament*, 6th ed. (Philadelphia: Westminster Press, 1961), vol. I, p. 276.

39. Ibid., p. 278.

40. Yehezkel Kaufmann, *The Religion of Israel* (Chicago: University of Chicago Press, 1960), p. 75.

41. Karl Barth, *The Doctrine of the Word of God* (New York: Charles Scribner's Sons, 1936), p. 157.

42. Barth, *Church Dogmatics*, vol. II, pt. 2, p. 712.

43. Ibid., vol. IV, pt. 3, pp. 446-447.

44. Ibid., vol. II, pt. 2, pp. 665f.

45. Soren Kierkegaard, *Fear and Trembling* (Princeton: Princeton University Press, 1952), p. 105. Emil Brunner's discussion of theological ethics in *The Divine Imperative* (New York: Macmillan, 1937), pp. 54ff. For Brunner eudaemonistic and "anthropocentric" conceptions of good have nothing to do with God's will to which alone the man of faith adheres.

46. John Stuart Mill, *An Examination of Sir William Hamilton's Philosophy* (New York: Library of Little Arts, 1867), pp. 119-129.

47. Ludwig Feuerbach, *The Essence of Christianity* (New York: Harper Torchbooks, 1957), app. 19, p. 320.

48. Martin Buber, *I and Thou* (New York: Charles Scribner's Sons, 1958), p. 78.

49. Ibid., p. 6.

50. Ibid., p. 78.

51. Ibid., p. 79.

52. Ibid., p. 83.

53. Martin Buber, *Mamre* (Melbourne: Melbourne University Press, 1946), p. 105.

54. Martin Buber, in "The Question to the Single One," *Between Man and Man* (London: Routledge & Kegan Paul, 1947), p. 78.

55. Maurice Friedman, *Martin Buber: The Life of Dialogue* (New York: Harper Torchbooks, 1960), p. 106.

56. Martin Buber, *Philosophical Interrogations*, ed. by Sidney Rome and Beatrice Rome (New York: Holt, Rinehart & Winston, 1964), p. 82.

57. Martin Buber, *Good and Evil* (New York: Charles Scribner's Sons, 1953), p. 142.

58. Martin Buber, *Eclipse of God* (New York: Harper Torchbooks, 1952), p. 105.

59. Martin Buber, "The Dialogue Between Heaven and Earth," in *Four Existentialist Theologians*, ed. Will Herberg (New York: Doubleday, 1958), pp. 202-203.

60. Ibid., p. 203.

61. Buber, "The Love of God and the Idea of Deity," in *Eclipse of God*, p. 49.

62. Ibid., p. 60.

63. Buber, *I and Thou*, p. 134.

64. Buber, *Eclipse of God*, p. 60.

65. Ibid.

66. Martin Buber, "The Two Foci of the Jewish Soul," in *The Writings of Martin Buber*, ed. Will Herberg (New York: Meridian Books, 1956), p. 269.

67. Martin Buber, "Religion and Philosophy," in *Eclipse of God*, p. 37.

68. Buber, *Philosophical Interrogations*, p. 92.

69. Buber, *Eclipse of God*, p. 96.

70. Ibid., p. 60.

71. Ibid., p. 97.

72. Buber, *I and Thou*, p. 135.

73. Ibid., p. 136.

74. Ibid., p. 8.

75. Ibid., p. 126.

76. Paul Schilpp and Maurice Friedman, eds., *The Philosophy of Martin Buber* (LaSalle, Ill.: Open Court, 1967), p. 10.

77. Buber, *Eclipse of God*, p. 119.

78. Ibid., p. 118.

79. Ibid.

80. Buber, *Philosophical Interrogations*, p. 92.

81. Buber, *Eclipse of God*, p. 50.

82. Moses Maimonides, *Guide of the Perplexed* I:56.

83. Ibid.

84. Barth, *Church Dogmatics*, vol. III, pt. 3, p. 426, on Psalm 36:5-7.

85. Isaiah 55:8.

86. Isaiah 55:10-11.

87. Hosea 11:9.

88. Mill, *Sir William Hamilton's Philosophy*, p. 130.

89. Romans, 1:19.

90. Hick, *Evil and the God of Love*, p. 98.

91. Ibid., pt. III.

92. Ibid., p. 202.

93. Ibid., p. 322.

94. Ibid., p. 323.

95. Ibid., pp. 359-360.

96. Nels Ferré, *Evil and the Christian Faith* (New York: Harper & Brothers, 1947), pp. 56ff.

97. Hick, *Evil and the God of Love*, p. 342.

98. John James, *Why Evil?* (London: Penguin Books, 1960), pp. 43f.

99. Hick, *Evil and the God of Love*, p. 370.

100. Ibid., p. 372.

101. Ibid., chap. 17, "The Kingdom of God and the Will of God."

102. Ezekiel 18:2, Jeremiah 31:29.

103. Hick, *Evil and the God of Love*, p. 385.

Chapter 6

1. Friedrich Nietzsche, *The Joyful Wisdom* (New York: Ungar Publishing Co., 1964), bk. V, sec. 357.

2. Immanuel Kant, *An Inquiry, critical and metaphysical, into the grounds of proof for the existence of God and into the theodicy*, trans. John Richardson (London, 1819).

3. Peter Berger, *The Sacred Canopy* (New York: Anchor Books, 1969), pp. 54ff.

4. Judah Halevi, *Kitab al Khuzari* (New York: Schocken Books, 1964), IV: 15.

5. Ibid.

6. Moses Maimonides, *Guide of the Perplexed*, I:54.

7. Ibid., III:13.

8. St. Thomas Aquinas, *Summa Theologica*, I, Q. 13, a. 2.

9. Ibid., Q. 13, a. 11.

10. F. C. Copleston, *Aquinas* (Baltimore: Penguin Books, 1955), p. 131.

11. Aquinas, *Summa Theologica* I, Q. 13, a. 11.

12. C. C. J. Webb, *God and Personality* (London: George Allen & Unwin, 1918), chap. II.

13. Karl Barth, *Church Dogmatics* (Edinburgh: T. & T. Clark, 1961), vol. II, pt. 1, p. 300.

14. Maimonides, *Guide of the Perplexed* III:13.

15. Ludwig Feuerbach, *The Essence of Christianity* (New York: Harper Torchbooks, 1957), p. 214.

16. Isaiah 45:19.

17. Feuerbach, *Essence of Christianity*, p. 260.

18. Ibid., p. 202.

19. Ibid., p. 10.

20. Ibid., p. 60.

21. Ibid., p. 153.

22. Deuteronomy 30:12-14.

23. George Berkeley, as quoted in G. J. Warnock's *Berkeley* (Baltimore: Pelican Books, 1953).

24. Gershom G. Scholem, *Major Trends in Jewish Mysticism* (New York: Schocken Books, 1946), pp. 11f.

25. Gershom G. Scholem, *Kabbalah* (New York: Quadrangle/New York Times Book Co., 1974), p. 88.

26. Mordecai M. Kaplan, *The Religion of Ethical Nationhood* (New York: Macmillan, 1970), p. 4; idem, *Questions Jews Ask* (New York: Reconstructionist Press, 1956), p. 103.

27. William Luitpen, *Phenomenology and Atheism* (Pittsburgh: Duquesne University Press, 1964), p. 219.

28. Charles Hartshorne, *Philosophers Speak of God* (Chicago: University of Chicago Press, 1953), p. 6.

29. Martin Heidegger, *Being and Time*, p. 51, quoted in Luitpen, *Phenomenology and Atheism*, p. 191.

30. John Dewey, *Experience and Nature* (Chicago: Open Court, 1925), p. 398.

31. Bertrand Russell, *The Problems of Philosophy* (London: Oxford University Press, 1948), p. 95.

32. Arthur Pap, *Elements of Analytic Philosophy* (New York: Macmillan, 1949), p. 35.

33. Hermann Cohen, *Religion of Reason* (New York: Frederick Ungar, 1972), p. 105.

34. Gilbert Ryle, *The Concept of Mind* (New York: Barnes & Noble, 1949), p. 16.

35. Ibid., p. 17.

36. John Dewey, *A Common Faith* (New Haven: Yale University Press, 1934), p. 22.

37. Ibid., p. 158.

38. Isaiah 5:20.

39. Talmud, *Yoma* 69b.

40. George Santayana, *Reason in Religion* (New York: Collier Books, 1962), p. 133.

41. Talmud, *Avodah Zarah* 54b.

42. Albert Camus, *The Rebel* (New York: Vintage Books, 1956), p. 20.

43. Carl Jung, *Answer to Job* (New York: Meridian Books, 1960), pp. 27ff.

Selected Bibliography

General

Berger, Peter. *The Sacred Canopy.* New York: Anchor Books, 1969.

Buber, Martin. *Between Man and Man.* London: Routledge & Kegan Paul, 1947.

Camus, Albert. *The Rebel.* New York: Vintage Books, 1956.

Cobb, John B., Jr. *Living Options in Protestant Theology.* Philadelphia: Westminster Press, 1962.

Ferré, Nels. *Evil and the Christian Faith.* New York: Harper & Brothers, 1947.

Flew, R. N. *The Idea of Perfection in Christian Theology.* London: Oxford University Press, 1934.

Hick, John. *Evil and the God of Love.* New York: Harper and Row, 1966.

James, John. *Why Evil?* Middlesex: Penguin Books, 1960.

Jonas, Hans. *The Gnostic Religion.* Boston: Beacon Press, 1963.

Lovejoy, Arthur O. *The Great Chain of Being.* New York: Harper & Brothers, 1960.

McCoy, Charles. "Theological Analysis." Unpublished manuscript. (Pacific School of Religion, Berkeley, 1968)

Marty, Martin. *Varieties of Unbelief.* New York: Holt, Rinehart & Winston, 1964.

Mascall, E. L. *The Secularization of Christianity.* New York; Holt, Rinehart & Winston.

Maslow, Abraham H. *Toward a Psychology of Being.* New York: D. Van Nostrand Co., 1962.

Niebuhr, H. R. *Radical Monotheism and Western Culture.* New York: Harper & Brothers, 1960.

Novak, Michael. *Belief and Unbelief.* New York: Macmillan, 1965.

Pike, Nelson. *God and Evil.* Readings edited by N. Pike. Englewood Cliffs, N.J.: Prentice-Hall, 1964.

Polanyi, Michael. *Personal Knowledge.* New York: Harper and Row, 1964.

Santayana, George. *Reason in Religion.* New York: Collier Books, 1962.

Schelling, F. W. J. *Of Human Freedom.* LaSalle, Ill.: Open Court, 1936.

Tsanoff, R. A. *The Nature of Evil.* New York: Macmillan, 1931.

Metaphysical Theodicy

The Classic Tradition

Aquinas, St. Thomas. *Basic Writings of Saint Thomas Aquinas.* Edited and annotated by Anton C. Pegis. 2 vols. New York: Random House, 1945.

Augustine, St. *Augustine: Confessions and Enchiridion.* Philadelphia: Westminster Press, 1953.

Leibniz, Gottfried Wilhelm. *Theodicy.* Don Mills, Ontario: J. M. Dent & Sons, 1966.

Lonergan, B. J. *Insight: A Study of Human Understanding.* London: Longman's,

Green & Co., 1958.

Maimonides, Moses. *Guide of the Perplexed.* New York: Hebrew Publishing Co., no date given other than translator's preface dated 1881.

Henry Nelson Wieman

The Source of Human Good, Carbondale: Southern Illinois University Press, 1946.

The Directive in History. Boston: Beacon Press, 1949.

The Empirical Theology of Henry Nelson Wieman. Edited by Robert Bretall. New York: Macmillan, 1963.

Charles Hartshorne

Man's Vision of God. Chicago: Willet, Clark & Co., 1941.

The Logic of Perfection. LaSalle, Ill.: Open Court, 1962.

Philosophers Speak of God. Edited with William Reese. Chicago: University of Chicago Press, 1953.

Paul Tillich

Systematic Theology. Chicago: University of Chicago Press, 1963.

Biblical Religion and The Search for Ultimate Reality. Chicago: University of Chicago Press, 1955.

Theology of Culture. New York: Oxford University Press, 1964.

Personalistic Theodicy

Aiken, Henry. *Reason and Conduct*. New York: Alfred A. Knopf, 1962.

Barth, Karl. *Church Dogmatics*. Edinburgh: T. & T. Clark, 1961.

__________. *The Doctrine of the World of God*. New York: Charles Scribner's Sons, 1936.

Brunner, Emil. *The Divine Imperative*. New York: Macmillan, 1937.

Buber, Martin. *I and Thou*. 2nd ed. New York: Charles Scribner's Sons, 1958.

____________. *Mamre*. Melbourne: Melbourne University Press, 1946.

____________. *Good and Evil*. New York: Charles Scribner's Sons, 1953.

____________. *The Eclipse of God*. New York: Harper Torchbooks, 1952.

Eichrodt, Walther. *Theology of the Old Testament*. 2 vols. 6th ed., Philadelphia: Westminster Press, 1961.

Friedman, Maurice. *Martin Buber: The Life of Dialogue*. New York: Harper Torchbooks, 1960.

Gollwitzer, Helmut. *The Existence of God as Confessed by Faith*. Philadelphia: Westminster Press, 1965.

Kaufmann, Yehezkel. *The Religion of Israel*. Chicago: University of Chicago Press, 1960.

Koehler, Ludwig. *Old Testament Theology*. London: Lutterworth Press, 1957.

Mill, John Stuart. *An Examination of Sir William Hamilton's Philosophy*. New York: Library of Little Arts, 1867.

Rome, Sidney, and Rome, Beatrice, eds. *Philosophical Interrogations*. New York: Holt, Rinehart & Winston, 1964.

Predicate Theology

Feuerbach, Ludwig. *The Essence of Christianity*. New York: Harper Torchbooks, 1957.

_________________. *The Principles of the Philosophy of the Future*. New York: Library of Liberal Arts, 1966.

Kant, Immanuel. *Critique of Practical Reason*. New York: Library of Liberal Arts, 1956.

Nietzsche, Friedrich. *The Joyful Wisdom*. New York: Ungar Publishing Co., 1964.

Index